Experiencing
REINCARNATION

Pen drawings by author
Cover art by Jane Evans

Experiencing
REINCARNATION

JAMES S. PERKINS

*This publication made possible
with the assistance of the Kern Foundation*

THE THEOSOPHICAL PUBLISHING HOUSE
Wheaton, Ill. U. S. A.
Madras, India/London, England

A Quest original. Fourth printing 1987

The Theosophical Publishing House
306 West Geneva Road
Wheaton, IL 60187

A publication of the Theosophical Publishing House, a department of the Theosophical Society in America.

Library of Congress Cataloging in Publication Data

Perkins, James Scudday.
    Experiencing reincarnation.
    (A Quest Book)
    Bibliography: p. Includes index.
    1. Reincarnation. I. Title.
BL515.P465   236   77-5249
       ISBN 0-8356-0500-0

Printed in the United States of America

The views set forth in this book are those of the author, compounded with knowledge gained from many theosophical and other sources, gratefully acknowledged.

CONTENTS

INTRODUCTION

Despite the fact that rhythmic recurrence of life is universal, and that cyclic growth is a natural cognizance of human consciousness, reincarnation as a concept of Man's perennial growth is not a generally accepted view in modern thought. Yet, no doctrine has a more imposing intellectual ancestry. That its rejection has been artificially imposed, and is not natural, is argued by the universal conformity of living creatures with Nature's cyclic performance.

The idea of reincarnation must have taken form when teaching began. Today, literature on the subject is extensive and indicative of further source-material regarding Man's knowledge that he both dies and lives again. Reincarnation can be traced far back into the sources of the great world religions and beyond, into primitive beliefs that fade into the night of time.

In modern days the idea receives little notice for the simple reason that people do not ordinarily have detailed memories of past lives on earth. Or, if they do, it is unusual to find anyone who is articulate about the matter. However, if a practical acceptance of reincarnation as a normal rhythm in Nature were to become widespread it would, no doubt, bring to light a submerged continent of personal testimony in support of this completely reasonable knowledge of Man's position, and the purposes he serves through life in the physical realm.

The veil to be lifted is that of memory, or rather the

nature of remembering. What is required is a clearer perception of the manner in which intra-life memories occur. For, despite the absence of objective brain memories, it can be shown that everyone does remember his past in unconscious ways, and is doing so all the time. A more penetrative attention to the character of remembering that occurs at different levels of consciousness, will help one to recognize and evaluate memories in one's own experience. Rather than expecting to gather memories of past lives, as one might remember past events when browsing through old albums of photographs, one should look for memories that occur in other, subtler forms.

What a perplexing world this would be if everyone awakened each morning with no recollection of his life yesterday. There would be no continuity to existence. Our lives without memory, could be likened to polyps on a coral reef. Yet, this would be an unfair comparison be-. cause everything everywhere does have memory of some kind, and every living creature has ongoing purpose. Each moment memory sums up the entire past in all organisms. In the foetus of every unborn baby in the mother's womb, a dramatic memory recapitulation takes place of the whole process of humanity's physical evolution. The summarizing doesn't stop at birth, it continues in man from moment to moment throughout life in all the levels of physical, emotional, and mental consciousness. At this instant we are the remembered essence of what we were in all of our yesterdays, plus that mysterious addition that is happening now and that arises from the future. Each morning sees the opening of an advance from where we were, to a new position. Yesterday's problems have been dealt with, and fresh strength has arrived to cope with those of today. This sense of progressive being and doing, of creating and enjoying, of reaching ahead and moving up, is measured in the convenient time patterns of yesterday, today and tomorrow. The nighttime gaps between the days are bridged by memory, and remembering preserves continuity through time.

Since the gap between night and day is bridged by memory, it follows logically that memory sustains continuity across the gaps of lifetimes on earth. The surrounding scene of our daily lives ought to alert us to a similarity between daytimes and lifetimes, and the parallel between those nightgaps that separate the days, and those other gaps that separate lifetimes. But the similarity does not seem to strike people forcibly except under extraordinary circumstances. When life becomes tortuous with pain, or boredom and ennui, when vision has disappeared in one's collapsing world, the stresses then impose sharper demands upon one to search for adequate answers to the deeper enigmas of life. Normally these questions do not disturb a person, and since memories of past lifetimes are not recognized as such, one remains unaware of the phenomenal rhythms in Nature that link everything in mysterious orbits, which for humanity are the cyclic movements termed reincarnation.

Undeniably cyclic growth is one of Nature's universal principles in evidence everywhere, from ocean tides to seasonal foliage. A much deeper perception, however, is required to discern the greater human orbit of reincarnation, because with it we have re-embodiment in physical form of an element in man that is deathless. This, then, is the knowledge that must be obtained: the deathlessness of Man.

In the following pages I am offering another approach to the subject: the attaining of an awareness of the cyclic law through observing the part that memory plays in threading our lifetimes together, thus illuminating the obscurities of reincarnation. One naturally shrinks from relating firsthand experiences, but these, for the writer, offer an authenticity beyond any other. So I am using memory experiences that forcibly stirred an awakening in me to this astonishing rhythm of life through which one recaptures what was known previously. In myself, fragments of memory later developed into a full conception of the great universal cycle of human rebirth. The events that I describe are autobiographical. But nothing can describe the spiritual freedom experienced with the realization that one is living immortally—now—as the law of reincarnation reveals when understood.

1

I RETURN FROM VIOLENT DEATH

The noon sky was brilliant that wintry day in March, 1948, as I walked along a country highway not far from the city of Chicago. A cold, gusty North-west wind was blowing, and I had the collar of my overcoat turned up around my ears. The wide highway was well constructed, and at this particular time, was devoid of traffic. Nevertheless, I was careful to walk along the grassy shoulder of the road on the side that faces traffic. Having just returned from a strenuous lecture tour that began in 1947, and included visits to England, Europe and the sub-continent of India, including new-born Pakistan—I was enjoying an unusual and infreqent moment of aloneness, peacefully content with the beauty surrounding me. At my place of residence no one knew that I was out for a brief walk and absent from the building. Feeling assured, therefore, of no disturbance for the present, I was in a completely placid state of meditation.

Without Warning

Meanwhile, far down the road, and entirely unknown to me, a motor car was swiftly approaching from the rear. Its driver had fallen asleep at the wheel, as he later admitted, and as was shown afterwards by the car tracks on the wet surface of the road. It may seem incredible that I heard nothing, and was utterly unaware of the car's approach; but the wind in the collar of my coat, together with my confident assurance regarding any traffic from the rear, as well as my absorption in other levels of consciousness, could account for the lapse of attention. As the car approached, it was veering across the width of the highway, and moving out upon the shoulder of the road behind me. Suddenly, with no note of warning whatsoever, the vehicle struck me with tremendous impact, shattering leg bones, and hurling me backward upon the radiator. The back of my head hit the car's hood with such a loud crack that the driver, (as I learned later) was startled awake, and instinctively jerked the wheel, jolting the car again onto the highway. This sudden twisting force catapulted my body onto the paved highway, landing it on the forehead and face.

Death While Meditating

After such a smash, and judging from all outer appearances, I was surely dead. Certainly, I had been expelled from my body in a most violent manner. Someone in a neighboring house heard the crash and the shriek of tires and called the police. An ambulance conveyed my body to a hospital where I remained unconscious for five days. The question was, whether or not I would live. So far as I was concerned, I had experienced death of my body while in full, free action. But, the compelling interest at this point was not the body; it was my state of consciousness. I experienced no period of blackout, of which I was conscious. There was no tumult in me of fear, horror, pain, or that numbing paralysis of ultimate disaster. The astonishing truth is that my stream of consciousness, which was engaged in meditation, was not interrupted at all! Whatever happened to the physical body occurred with no attention given to it. My awareness remained focussed in the abstract regions I had entered while walking peacefully along the road prior to the accident. The continuity of my mental pursuit remained unbroken during, and following, the violent change in my physical condition. This experience, it seems to me, has unusual significance regarding the importance of the state of mind just prior to, and during, the time of death. There have been many instances of people "experiencing death" and recollecting the nature of their last moments. Some have even brought back memories of what life seemed to them to be on the other side. But I believe the experience I am describing is unique, because the dreadful occurrence took place while I was in a state of meditation. I remained undisturbed, without any ripple of anxiety, because no warning factors were present. Then, what followed suggests that an extraordinary opportunity is offered at one's death-hour for an intelligent approach to the experience.

Into The All And The Alone

I did become gradually aware that a change had taken place, but it seemed of only incidental importance, as though my coat had fallen to the floor, while I was engaged in some absorbing preoccupation. What was important was the expansion of consciousness that opened horizons vaster than any I had ever before experienced. Indeed, the expansion was overwhelming. I seemed suddenly directly related with everything in existence, and completely devoid of any sense of time and space. Awareness focussed upon a Source of Life from which radiated forces flowing

7

into everything, as though the cosmic projection of the universe is ceaselessly taking place at high velocity, and everything is participating in the action. All of this is veiled in the profoundest mystery, experienced as an awareness, rather than as something shown, or revealed to me. It was not as though in a dream—not dissociated from my self-system, but identified with it. I was simply *there*, firmly centered in what must be thought of as an 'All-Self', because it was consciously within the body of All. It seemed there was no need of an individual form or body! This state of being continued throughout the five days that the physical body, and physical brain were immobilized and inert. "I" remained consciously alive, freely and happily oriented as described.

The bond with the physical body had not been entirely severed. I found that I could return to the physical plane partially, if necessary. I did so on occasions, and delivered messages through my body to the nurse who happened to be present. Apparently, the brain was usable to a limited extent, but from another base. I certainly dwelt apart from it. Whenever there was such use, consciousness immediately withdrew afterwards to that inmost realm, where it seemed now to be resident. Throughout the five days that I remained thus located, I was in undisturbed contemplation of the transcendence described, an awareness of which was taking place in me, in some way. It was characterized by a radiant union of beneficence; not as though I were in some isolated condition of detached intellectual inspection. Union with the All-ness seemed immune to hindrance. Were it not for this consciousness of unity, of Self-identity with the Whole, I would have experienced an awesome loneliness. I could have asked, where were all the people? Was no one else around? But the central characteristic of the experience was identification with all of life, with no necessity for graduated differences in persons, forms, and objects.

The Emptiness Potential

From this contemplation there arose an awareness of my own limitations. The transcendence that I seemed to be experiencing did not shut out perception of the awesome regions of emptiness in human consciousness. This emptiness I now beheld. The empty levels in myself are there because I have yet to reach unfoldment in those areas. I clearly knew that the awakening and fulfillment of these levels will require future evolutionary growth through many relationships with which I am yet to be identified. These relationships and situations will ultimately draw forth every potential of love, wisdom and power, that is to be unfolded. How precious, then, becomes every relationship in life, with family and kin, with friends and strangers, with companions, and business associates, with institutions and duties, with those kindly disposed and with difficult people as well. Each situation in life evokes some additional aspect of one's nature, some new depth in one's capacity to understand and to act upon creatively.

Thirst For Renewed Limitation

As these realizations became intensely clear, there was an urge reborn in me—the thirsting to renew sentient experience, as though there was unfinished business to resolve, undeveloped powers awaiting attention in the great schoolroom of the physical world. The urge to return to transitory experience drew me inexorably again into the physical form. The movement downward was a definite action from "there" to "here". Consciousness became oriented to the necessity for limitation in worlds below—the need for boundaries that one could deal with—for confinement within what one could see and feel and know objectively. A newborn baby has the boundaries of the crib; the inclosure itself stimulates recognition, comprehension, and creative response. The walls of limitation for an adult are the whole wide world, and beyond. Even the Solar Logos can create only within a frame of limitation. Limitation is inevitable; orderly growth could not take place without it.

Re-entry To Earth Life

I could no more resist the tidal drift back into the limitations of physical life, than can a leaf floating over Niagara Falls. The experience was essentially that of reincarnation in miniature, a descent through mental and astral levels that ultimately reached the veils of etheric awareness—the portals through which one passes into physical form. Here I experienced the 'waters of Lethe', or the '*Nepenthean* veil' of forgetfulness that curtains off the flow of inner consciousness to and from brain consciousness. Through it I passed, slipping into full, agonized awareness of my physical body's condition. It was a passage into brain and body consciousness that was a dreadful shock. The experience of conscious re-entry was as though a thick blanket of fog was instantly drawn around my entire system of information, blurring the inner-outer lines of communication. For me, it was a blotting out of the infinite horizons that had opened.

Upon resumption of physical life, my first most notable impression was of the complete beguilement to which the human being is subjected in his physical confinement. We truly are shackled by the brain-consciousness, with all values fundamentally distorted. It was only with the greatest effort that I could arouse interest in pursuing normal lines of worldly activity. With reluctance I undertook existence again in physical form, knowing now of realities that lie beyond the deceptive screen of materiality—knowing that "I" am certainly not the physical body. I could never again be completely deceived by the convic-

10

tion that physical life is all that there is for me, or for anyone else.

Free Of The Death-Fiction

My attitude towards death changed forever. The ultimate fate of the physical body could no longer be a matter of fearful concern. I was aware of a new freedom, a certain liberation from the dominance of the physical body over mind and soul. I had first-hand knowledge that the expanded Self-consciousness that lies outside the physical barricades, is my *real* Self; and that in those regions beyond the body and the mind, ultimate freedom and bliss are known. The whole fabrication of fears about death, I could now see, is a wicked, fictitious delusion that is propagated and sustained by man's own ignorance.

One feature of this experience continues with me; that is the remarkable fact that some part of my consciousness remains oriented to that exalted region and continues to provide a mystical pathway for inward exploration, and it holds ever before me the challenge of those empty areas that are yet to be unfolded. This strange faculty for going *there* and returning *here,* remains as a resource for intuitive flashes on my horizon of awareness.

The Reincarnation Question

Implications arising from this experience just related, have posed questions that would be too baffling to enter into, were I without some knowledge of reincarnation, and the occult side of Man's nature. I've had to ask myself, first of all, in what respects I find this experience to be actually an example in miniature of the great cycle of reincarnation? I can trace clearly some illuminating parallels between what I experienced, and what is known of the full, normal cycle. I have had to decipher just *where* in the universal regions of consciousness I happened to go.

11

There was no astral plane experience, such as those usually associated with the after-death state, nor did I seem to be in any mental locale that was recognizable. There were no people around me, no angels of any kind, no teachers, gods, or anthropomorphic God, present. This aspect of no peopling raises most profound and serious questions of all, while at the same time, it points toward the most inspiring of the revelations connected with the entire episode.

These, as well as other implications and questions relative to them will be developed throughout the chapters of this book. It will also include questions about reincarnation that have been asked many times, such as:

Is it possible to 'prove' reincarnation?

If my personality, as I know it to be, dies and does not reincarnate, just *what* does?

Why do I not remember previous lifetimes?

Isn't reincarnation most unjust if my present life must suffer for actions by 'somebody else'—the personality that was my last life?

Do people reincarnate immediately?

How long will I be dead?

Where do I go in the meantime?

Does reincarnation go on forever?

When did it start?

What caused it?

What terminates it?

If I am to be reborn, will I continue to be the same sex as I am now?

Do human beings ever reincarnate in animal forms?

With this knowledge of reincarnation, what is the intelligent attitude, and approach, to death—to life?

If reincarnation is true, why should I make any effort to struggle against adversity or to overcome handicaps, when I can wait for a better birth in happier circumstances?

Do families as a group reincarnate together?

How can reincarnation be reconciled with population growth?

Why is there so much disorder, injustice, and suffering in the world—must we return to this state of affairs endlessly?

Does reincarnation support the concept that supreme order reigns throughout the universe?

Why is there so much confusion and contradictory information regarding reincarnation?

Why has there been so little intellectual attention given to this universal law, which, if it is true, and taught as an intelligent approach to the problems of life, would alter the outlook of every human being on this planet?

2

REMEMBERING REINCARNATION

Memory is an essential function in Nature's operation. The universe apparently is recording its manifestation. The whole of life in all of its kingdoms is registering a total memory of experience everywhere. As will be shown more fully later, the universal recording takes place at the most subtle level of consciousness in the universe, and is not to be conceived as something in the nature of a cosmic photograph album. At that level of consciousness, time does not exist; past, present and future, are merged in a ceaseless "Now" awareness. This *now* consciousness is extraordinarily different from our sequential existence. For example, memory of the future is as available as that of the past! The manifestation of the universe is a now happening. But the total memory experience is available only to liberated Adepts,* those who have become qualified to use it lawfully. The discovery of means by which the enlightenment can be reached is one of the more profound possibilities before us.

---

*Perfected human beings.

Memory Systems In Nature

This abstract aspect of universal memory may be viewed more simply from our time-sequential standpoint, as Nature summarizing the essentials of life in everything everywhere at all times. There is not only a summarizing process but a continuous review in operation. No moment is possible, for men as well as other creatures, when there is not a recollecting of the past unfolding in all regions of being. It is as though there are cosmic systems of memory-computerization and recovery functioning ceaselessly. Memory-banks are being stored in every creature in Nature. The recovery goes on in the atoms, in the cells, the organs and bodies. In all instinctive actions of animals and man, we see memory arising from past experience and dominating the course of action at the moment. Individual creatures of the lower kingdoms are ever sharing experience in common pools of intelligence where it is being transformed into instinct, to become the heritage of other, later, individual members of that species. In each species, the many individual units are merged in single group-intelligences; through these, each individual member benefits from the experiences of the whole group. Just how all these activities take place is a part of the knowledge about the subtler regions of the universe, and the lawful evolution of creatures. This is an enormous subject, but its study opens avenues of extraordinary understanding regarding the nature of the universe and Life's evolution in it.

Memory As Re-experiencing

Higher organisms, such as man, contain within their individual self-systems, storages of memory that are outside of—and beyond—the reach of normal mentality. Despite this apparent remoteness, the storages do exist and are contactable. It is from this source that occasionally there flashes a pattern of memory so vivid that it becomes a compelling influence in the conscious mind, literally constituting a *re-experiencing* of the basic features of some past event. Such a recovery of memory can have a life-changing impact upon an individual. It was through this kind of an experience that I made my first approach to a knowledge of reincarnation.

I believe that many persons have flashes of memory of this kind, and that such recoveries are straight out of past lifetimes on this earth. People generally are hesitant to speak of such personal experiences, because being out of the ordinary, they tend to denote an uncomfortable strangeness in an individual. Yet, this kind of memory may be a more reliable source of evidence of the truth of reincarnation, than are the sensate memories being sought today as proofs of it. These 'proofs' are generally based on remembered facts by someone whose last lifetime was recent enough for the facts to be adequately verified historically and geographically. But we shall see as we examine the normal full cycle of reincarnation, that such testimonials offered as proof of reincarnation may tend to cloud the realities of the great cycle, casting an unreal, and often objectionable obscuration upon the grandeur of its meaning and purpose.

Memory From Outside The Conscious Mind — 3 Classifications

True memory is so easily confused with wishful thinking, or speculation, or other delusive factors, that the individual can discriminate between the true and the false only with the assistance of his intuition. However, there are certain tests for validity that can be applied. For example, the validity of a memory-experience can be determined by its effect upon one's life. A true memory has the quality of *re-experiencing* what was known before, rather than merely recollecting something that hap-

16

pened in the past. It will *endure;* and not fade. It will *grow* in its effect upon one's basic outlook; it will become *life-shaping.* Memory experiences that arise from outside the conscious mind, can be classified under three headings, with respect to their sources.

These three classifications, as I see them, are: (1) *Continuous Memory*—which is ceaselessly arising, mostly unconsciously, out of the material nature of everyone. (2) *Immortal Memory*—arising out of the reincarnated immortal Self who actually experienced the past as an individual, and recorded it in the non-dying 'Causal' body. (3) *Cosmic Memory*—stemming from the profoundest sources of Man's being. This memory is rare, and recoverable only through the most exalted circumstances of meditation and insight. Extraordinary individuals such as the true seers of the world, the great teachers, saints and heroes, have benefited mankind with their cosmic memories.

Continuous Memory

As noted, memory is occurring all of the time in every living organism, including man in his many levels of being. The exploitation of continuous memory as a source of reincarnational evidence could be developed widely; its fields are open to anyone, for unlimited investigation. Extensions of it are already in use, for example, in industrial processes today, where 'memory' in metals and chemical elements is useful to manufacturers. Biology, as well as all other sciences of life offer fields of further evidence.

Great horticultural scientists such as Luther Burbank, George Washington Carver, and many others in various countries of the world, have produced astonishing— almost magical—results through communication with plants and their strange faculty of memory. That plants "talk" and feel love and hate, seems undeniable, when

17

reading of the life and works of Luther Burbank, whose feats with plants are well known. He once said, while conducting experiments with cacti, "I talked to them to create the vibration of love."* He took them into his confidence, and assured them that, "you have nothing to fear". And, of all his plants, he said "when they talk, I listen.**

Plants Have Memory

Experiments by Russian scientists indicate effectively that *"plants have memory"*, "they can feel pain". "They cry out! Plants remember everything!" One learned member of the Soviet Academy of Science working in a Siberian Research Center stated that, "We had a man molest, even torture a geranium for several days in a row. He pinched it, tore it, pricked its leaves with a needle, dripped acid on its living tissues, burned it with a lighted match, and cut its roots. Another man took tender care of the same geranium, watered it, worked its soil, sprayed it with fresh water . . . and treated its burns and wounds. When they electroded their instruments to the plant in the presence of the 'torturer' the "recorder of the instrument began to go wild. The plant didn't just get 'nervous', it was afraid, it was horrified. If it could have, it would have either thrown itself out of the window, or attacked its torturer." When the 'good' man came near the plant, and the 'torturer' went away, the graph died down, the "recorder traced out smooth—one might almost say *tender*—lines on the graph".***

It has been shown that plants can share water with a deprived neighbor. The sensitivity of life in the vegetable kingdom is becoming well documented. A growing variety

*"Secret Life of Plants," - P. Tompkins & C. Bird - p. 123.

**Ibid. p. 123.

***Ibid. p. 73-4.

18

of investigations reveal how marvellous are the occult wonders in Nature around us.

As for memory in animals, there are endless examples, with no need to question its obvious operation. Animals have a remarkable memory capability, as shown in every effort to train them. The study of animal instincts opens the surprising extent of their memory faculty.

Man Has Continuous Memory

Students of reincarnation become familiar with references that support the conception of continuous memory across recurring lifetimes. Among the more well-known instances is that of the astounding performances of the child Mozart, which seem to have no other sensible explanation. How could this child at seven years of age possibly have composed sonatas, and oratorios at eleven, while another individual grown to adulthood, having practiced the piano for many years, can hardly produce an acceptable rendition of Mozart's music? Is not the more reasonable answer to this question, that Mozart, the person, was a reincarnated individual who had devoted several lifetimes principally to music? Doubtless, every hour of the day in Mozart's life on earth, saw a continuous recovery of his musical faculty. This kind of recovery is quite definitely an example of remembering the past in terms of re-experiencing and continuing it.

We see all around us people who, for instance, seem to have a natural mechanical faculty regarding machinery. They are born mechanics, with an immediately practical approach to a faulty engine, that presents to the rest of us only a baffling enigma. Extraordinarily competent people are examples of continued use of a faculty that was developed in some other lifetime. Have you ever noticed that almost everyone quickly and easily picks up the various skills of civilized life? On the other hand, there are some people who do not. There is no clear accounting for their deficiency until you apply the theory of reincarnation. Upon investigation you are apt to find that the so-called backward people have a ready instinct, and superior skills of another kind that could only have been acquired through incarnations in other Races that perhaps are not at the forefront of modern civilization, where more sophisticated skills are being developed.

How is it that nearly everyone recognizes a friend or enemy instantly? Why do some people become immediately addicted to intoxicating liquor, or some other drug, or vice? Why do certain people become confirmed alcoholics so quickly, while the vast majority of people can use alcohol moderately, or do without it altogether? When a person who has suffered this affliction in a past life takes his first drink in this lifetime, even as a child, a warning bell sounds in him, and he knows, or should realize, that danger lies in that direction. We say, 'conscience' warns him. But one's so-called conscience is the Soul's memory of mistakes made in the past. This is another manifestation of continuous memory through re-experience. Wherever you look, in every direction, you find people who are natural executives, engineers, artists, military professionals, ministers, administrators, teachers, they are continuing along a line of recall in which memory from the past is shaping their present lifetime. We do not notice this class of continuous memory as such, because we are using it all the time; it is just a part of life in general. But if one recognizes the law of reincarnation, and begins to be aware of the flow of memory from the past as continuous in daily life, new pages of revelation open every day, that become added documentation of the reality of this great rhythm in Nature, reincarnation.

Immortal Memory

It is when we meet an experience of memory that is almost as vivid as a stroke of lightning, that we awaken to the realization that such memory has extraordinary and profound meaning for us, and we must try to adjust our outlook accordingly. I have classified the experiencing of such impacts as the recovery of *Immortal Memory*. This kind of memory offers the firmest evidence of all, I believe, as to the truth of reincarnation, because the memory grows increasingly influential in giving direction to one's present lifetime. Its influence will have a *correctional* quality that acts as though it came through some 'feedback' function in man's mysterious self-system. It is almost as if an obscure memory of some past episode or trend is arising again to guide the course of one's present situation in life, particularly if it is at a crucial juncture. The effect of an immortal memory is *life-shaping*; it is not only durable, but grows in depth as a central guiding factor in one's life.

In clarifying this explanation, I will illustrate it with three examples drawn from personal experience, that together were actually the steps of my personal approach to the knowledge of reincarnation.

An Instance of Immortal Memory

My first experience of immortal memory occurred when I visited an art museum for the first time. I was totally unprepared for what happened. My boyhood and schooling had been spent in a small country town where there were no such cultural facilities as art galleries and museums. In 1918 I had left my home to enlist in the U.S. Army, in World War I. And now, two years later, I was attending a university course in civil engineering, alternating school studies with outdoor labor as a structural-steel worker, and later as a railway hand in a section gang. Art had not played a part in my life. Yet, when I entered a museum for the first time, and stood in the presence of collection of paintings and drawings, I felt a strange and growing excitement. The faint aroma of oil paints aroused a queer sense of familiarity with this environment, as though somehow, somewhere, I had known it before! But I had had no such experience in this life. *Where* could such a familiarity have come from? *When* could I possibly have gained it? Certainly not in my present life. Yet here I was, imaginatively experiencing a hitherto unknown delight in the creation of beauty through drawing and painting. Scarcely having laid aside the tools of heavy labor, it didn't seem plausible that I could be thus suddenly awakened to a familiarity with color arrangement and design, and with such a strong attraction to representational drawing. How does one instantly become knowingly appreciative of the technique of oil painting, of that dexterity of brushwork that skillfully suggests the sharp planes and full rounded form of a head and face in a portrait? I stood enthralled in the grip of an awareness that I had opened a fresh page in my life. Something very real had appeared, that had been entirely absent until now. I did not in the least understand how this unveiling of consciousness could be happening. Many years later I could ask, "Was I *remembering* experiences known in some past life?" The recalling was not factual, as though remembering some house in which I had lived, or what clothes I wore—not the satisfying details of 'when'—and 'how'—or 'what'—that usually one may expect in the way of memory. But, there was a certainty of awareness that was not to be denied. Not only had I known these wondrous experiences before, but obviously I was *re-experiencing* them now! The incidentals of that mysterious past did not concern me; what mattered was the fact that yesterday this world of beauty and reality was entirely unknown to me, and today I was possessed to an amazing degree of subtle first-hand knowledge, of a new world, and its magic properties. The experience could not be put down to a momentary flight of fantasy because, as I found later, it *endured* and it *grew*. Some inner door had definitely opened—some expansion of consciousness had taken place.* So clearly did I realize it that a fundamental change in my outlook and aims became imperative. Thus the recall became *life-shaping*. Due to that experience and its cumulative effect, the inescapable conclusion grew, that I had to abandon the idea of becoming an engineer. It was under this compulsion that I found it necessary to turn seriously to Art—preferably the art of painting, as a life pursuit.

Looking back upon the experience after many years of study and self-exploration in the fields of consciousness, I am now perfectly clear that I was experiencing the impact of a body of memory from the past. It was remembering the only way that has validity as a bona fide recall, which is to say, through consciously *re-experiencing the essentials of what was known in another lifetime*. This is the first phase. The second, and more important phase, is the growing reality and sense of direction that a flashback provides in the present. In me, continuous memory began, which resulted in a rapid recovery of art skills that could only have been developed in a former incarnation.

Although I had inadvertently recovered the essential quality of an experience from another lifetime, I did not connect it with any concept of reincarnation, because I had never heard of the term, as far as I am aware. Certainly the idea had not occupied my conscious thought. Even in the midst of the experience, I was not preoccupied with ideas as to how I could be 'remembering'—if it was memory. The all-important fact was the experiencing of this hitherto unknown area of my consciousness that was now becoming rapidly familiar to me. The re-experiencing element gave the memory validity, which was further strengthened by the durable, and life-shaping features that together, attest to its genuineness.

It can be observed that the essential experiences of a

*It is in the light of this experience that I attribute the genius of Mozart to efforts made in past lifetimes.

23

past life are sometimes close to the surface of one's present waking consciousness, and readily 'felt' even if not specifically recalled. For example, certain salient aspects of an experience of death by drowning under fearful and tragic circumstances in a recent lifetime, may have been so vividly impressed in the individual's memory bank that these aspects might well be recalled as a strong antipathy if not positive dread of being in, or on, large bodies of water, even though no objective memory whatsoever exists of an actual episode of drowning. The fact that innumerable people experience in various ways this kind of 'memory', is but further evidence of its universality. When you multiply this kind of instance by the numerous other ways in which such memories occur, you begin to realize that everyone is remembering the past always, even though unaware of it. The recapture of knowledge itself, is but remembering. Plato and other thinkers have said as much.

But my education in reincarnation had only begun. A year after the first experience, a second episode of a different character occurred.

A Second Episode—The Mystery Deepens

The second experience of immortal memory was concerned with a more directly personal relationship. It happened in the art department of an advertising agency. Out of nowhere, with the first instant of meeting, I 'remembered' my future wife. She was an utter stranger five minutes before she walked through the door of that studio, in which I was art director. The opening of that door precipitated another incredible experience of recall. The remembering had nothing to do with her person or appearance. This was not an instant biological attraction. As before, it had that same strange inward quality, as though I was awake in some immortal area of my being that spanned the gap between today and that other time when this experience had happened before. Inwardly, I found that the essential beingness in this other person who had now entered my life, was as familiar to me as was my own. Yet, how could this be true? How can two strangers native to two entirely different social backgrounds and geographical regions become instantly aware of their *essential unity* and likeness, were it not that they had known each other in close relationship in some other cycle of time?

With this new experience in remembering, the seriousness of the whole question of recurring earth-lives was beginning to press upon me. Had this person and I been associated together in some former lifetime, and had now met again? I had no answer to this baffling puzzle. Up until this point I had encountered no knowledge or theory of reincarnation. Only a year had elapsed since my first experience of this kind. But the mystery was growing into deep questioning, and my search for answers was intensifying, and I was becoming disquieted. A fresh aspect that appeared in this second incident was that of foreknowledge. In some strange way I was aware from the first instant of meeting my wife-to-be, that ours was a *predestined* path together in this lifetime. Once more I knew that this instant-memory could not be classed as fantasy, because it, too, had a *life-shaping* impact. Its influence *endured* and *grew* throughout the three years of adjustment required for the decision that resulted finally in changing the course of our two individual lives, uniting them henceforth. That door was opened over 50 years ago, and our paths have continued together ever since.

With this second episode, I became much more alert to things remembered, or anticipated, due to some faint overshadowing of memory. For example, in my youth I had never seen a snowstorm, or a mountain, or a huge surf on an ocean beach, but the very thought of these aspects of Nature aroused a growing anticipation of encountering them *'again'*. Experiencing them 'again' would be familiar to me. I could look forward eagerly to renewing acquaintance with these exciting natural features.

On the other hand, I was aware also of things that *should have grown in familiarity,* but actually did the reverse. Certain fundamental relationships, such as my inherited religion, were not growing closer to me. Instead, from early youth the religion I was born into had faded, as though it were being vaguely supplanted by faint recollections of some other way of viewing the ultimates of life; although I could not quite recapture consciously what that other outlook could be. I felt increasingly alienated from the theological doctrines, and the ethical and moral practices based on them. In fact, the more I enquired into the history of religion, the more serious became my doubts as to the veracity in general, of pronouncements made. I was somehow faintly aware of the existence of other approaches to Truth, other terms in which Reality could be experienced, especially with respect to the ultimate fate of Man. What those other terms were remained obscure and undefinable. Anyone who has ever become aware that essential knowledge about the universe is in one's mental vicinity—almost within grasp, yet somehow out of reach—will understand what I mean. Actual contact with it eluded every effort in my search. This reaching for something that was 'there' and yet 'not there' became for me a mounting disturbance with its insistent demands. The search for answers intensified into a paramount preoccupation that finally culminated in a third experience of immortal memory.

A Third Episode—The Awakening

As though born of necessity, the intermittent but persistent search through libraries at long last led me to a small volume of Theosophy that described exactly what I desperately needed to learn — the puzzling connections between the known self and that unknown part of me, of which I was nebulously aware but could not grasp in the terms at my command. The little book remedied my need immediately. It opened the doors of recognition, by presenting, for one thing, a simple but comprehensive explanation of the full cycle of reincarnation, together with its enlightenment as to man's nature. Equally important, this book was my introduction to that principle of causation that for ages in Eastern thought has been recognized as *Karma*. These two doctrines—reincarnation and karma—perceived together, are as dual aspects of a single universal principle, which can be formulated as a *rhythmic return to equilibrium*. This perception signalled for me the sunrise of intelligence upon life's darkest enigmas. With these explanations, I climbed the great mountain of knowing and beheld the truth that universal order does prevail, that justice is eternal, and that lawfulness brings back to balance, across every span of time, all forces that are generated and released in this universal scheme. For the first time in this life I recovered the sense of direction. With Nietzsche I felt that in every cycle of human life there comes an hour when one perceives the eternal recurrence of things; that "everything goeth, everything returneth", and order is ceaselessly restored, whatever the calamities manufactured by man.

With the full impact of these two concepts—the cyclic recurrence of human life through reincarnation, and its twin doctrine of cause and consequence, otherwise known as karma—unshakably interwoven into my outlook, a continuous process of enlightenment began. On every side objects, incidents, events, situations, appearances and disappearances, seemed to reveal further evidences of the truth before me. Life itself poured forth boundless documentation. Additional readings upon the subject hastened the mounting structure of wholeness. To reincarnation and karma was added the element of *cosmic purpose*. And the great question was answered: To what end does this 'changing world and changeless law' ever move? Clearly, reincarnation and karma are the changeless laws, by means of which Man accomplishes his spiritual evolution into Superman. The cyclic movement spirals upward; the rhythmic growth is an unleashing of hidden potentials ever unfolding toward perfection. The growth of the Soul is directed to attainment of the fullness of the stature of divinity that has been existent from the beginning. Man unerringly becomes God.

With this triple awareness, the tensions of ultimate anxieties began to relax in me, and I could now look with assurance back upon the lowlands and bogs of my ignorance of these matters, and to marvel at the immeasurable past that has led me to this plateau of serene knowing.

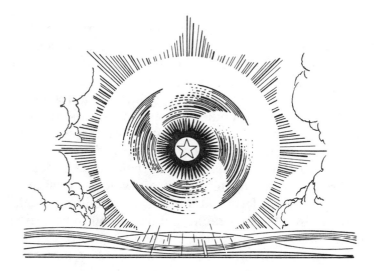

3

DEEPER WELLS OF MEMORY

The assembling of all major elements of the Ancient Wisdom (that I had now recognized) were becoming firmly embedded in the foundations of my outlook. The steadiness of conviction that grew in me of the deeper truths which I attribute to memory of another kind. It is as though this memory comes from profounder levels than those of immortal consciousness. Because of its nature, I have classified these deeper recalls as *Cosmic Memory*. Its recovery begins with a growing sensitivity and response to the eternal aspects in Nature, what we refer to as the voice of Reality. Cosmic memory also arises from contemplating ancient and heroic scriptures regarding the eternal and universal truths. Anyone, without erudition or even wide learning, may experience Reality listening to the primeval music of Nature.

Cosmic Remembering

Walking along an ocean shore, listening to the rhythm of the sea, one hears the same timeless singing in oneself. There are many mnemonic features in Nature, sustained through the ages, that enable one to awaken cosmic memory. Ocean surf has a rhythm and sound that has remained characteristic through endless aeons. Many times in past incarnations it must have been vigorously impressed upon our consciousness. Perhaps that message is the fascination the sea holds for us. One reaches wordless depths of awareness listening to the magic voices of Nature. Whoever has sat quietly watching the great billows breaking far out from some beach, and has noted the cresting ranks of lesser waves rolling steadily landward, until at last they are but rippling tides of foam reaching far up the sands, laying at one's feet little castles of gleaming bubbles, must have received them appreciatively as messages from the sea. Each bubble, with its rainbow hues reflecting the great heavens and all of space, are as little crystal balls of memory calling one to other ages, other times, other loves that were written in the language of sand, and surf, and sea.

Similarly does the sigh of wind in the trees, or out upon the vast grasslands, speak a language of cosmic memory. There is a music in the great mountains that utterly beguiles one's attention from market mediocrity. It is heard in the twilight and the break of day in lofty, lonely mountains, and out upon their primeval ramparts, calling with a poignancy that wrings utmost emotional response in those who hear it. And at night, watching the awesome costume of the sky, the star constellations in their march across the heavens bring awareness of the infinite spans of time and distance that we have gazed upon repeatedly in other incarnations. In such ways, the heavy shell of our mortal encasement grows thin, and a *knowing* awakens that was never learned in the schools of this clamorous, unseeing era.

I discovered the essentials of reincarnation borne out in numberless ways in Nature; and out of the observations grew the certainty that memory is the basis of seeing and knowing. I began to wonder about deeper wells of memory that must exist in the larger bodies of humanity. Do nations and races of mankind as entities, hold a wealth of memory that will aid the recovery of Truth? Does each of Nature's different departments, as such, have its own memory bank?

Do Nations of People Remember?

It is not a mere guess that nations do reincarnate. The idea is a reasonable extension of the substantiated fact that families and small groups of people reincarnate together. Extraordinary people, such as great statesmen, great explorers and pioneers, great warriors and geniuses, seem to arrive on earth together, and are associated with special developments of civilization in their time. A good example is the group of geniuses that lived during the Golden Age in Greece, who, it is said, reappeared as a group during the Renaissance in Europe. The mystics and saints who were present on earth during the birth of Christianity, apparently returned in medieval Europe to strengthen the growth of that religion. And when Western Civilization was ready for expansion, history records the lives and acts of great explorers, pioneers, statesmen and warriors, who appeared with their specialized faculties as though coming when needed in the unfolding of civilization. Nations of people are bound together by mystical ties that cement their loyalties; they tend to reincarnate together in the spiralling growth of unique national character.

Thus we may find reasonableness in the observation that the might and majesty of Rome as a collective unit of individuals, with a special national characteristic that set them apart, reincarnated as the British people who established the world-encircling British Empire, with its center in Britain, its governing body pinpointed in London. And again, if we look further, it was not only the character of the ancient city of Athens, but its luminous creative spirit, that reincarnated in the graceful and enlightened atmosphere of Paris, and of France. These statements may be thought of as flights of imagination, yet there are significant parallels that indicate the spiralling growth of these bodies through the reincarnating groups that we classify as nations. Nations are really schools on earth, attended by individuals for some particular development available therein. Patterns of history seem to repeat themselves in remarkable ways. Nations and their leaders reincarnate, recycling the old circumstances in new frames, as though reincarnation brings repeatedly another chance, and yet another.

A Remarkable Memory in 1938

Lending credence to this view, so far as I am concerned, are the memory episodes that occurred in me as a series of dreams, in 1938. At the time, it will be recalled, the German military might, under Hitler, was toppling the scales of peace and war toward the certainty of German territorial expansion in Europe through military aggression. No one living at that time will forget the appeasement efforts of the British Government to stem the threatening moves of the German Reich; nor, in particular, that famous episode when the Prime Minister, Mr. Neville Chamberlain, returned from Berchtesgarten waving the non-aggression document signed by Herr Hitler and himself, supporting his declaration to the British people that, "we shall have peace in our time". The exultant message stands as a landmark of political irony—of high hopes dashed by reality.

Many extraordinary occult forces surrounded and played upon that strange, unpredictable personage, Adolf Hitler. Obviously he was one of those enigmatic points that appear at times in history, around which the fate of the world swings on its course toward higher destiny, or doom. Such individuals seem to stand as implacable pillars, that split the highway of human progress, surrounding it with clouds of confusion, posing the sphinx-like question: "How, now, will mankind fare forth?" At such points, momentous decisions must be made that affect the course of the human race.

The first of the dreams took place one night in 1938: I seemed to be with a particular group of people who visited Hitler, believing it possible to point out to him the consequences involved under the karmic law, of his unleashing terrible forces of destruction upon the world. One by one, each of our group had an audience with Hitler in his great hall seated behind his impressive desk. I had no idea of what the others had spoken about, but I intended specifically to ask him if he knew of the existence of the Brotherhood of Adepts who administer the forces of good and evil that humanity releases upon itself, balancing these toward man's welfare, with the greater forces of destiny that determine the ongoing course of evolution? Hitler replied that he not only knew of Them, but that he was serving the Plan! "You see," he said, "I *am* the Will of the German people, I must do my duty to the end." And he conducted me to a demonstration of what he meant. We were on a platform in the great stadium at Nuremburg. Thousands of German citizens were arranged in their seats, tier upon tier around the stadium, listening with enthralled rapture to the speech Hitler was making. He ended with a mighty "Sieg Heil!" which brought a roaring response of "Sieg Heil!" from the crowd. With that, he stepped forward on the platform, continuing his speech, then gave another "Sieg Heil!" After several of these

stridings forward, he reached the edge of the platform—
which stood some 18 ft.- 20 ft. high. Without hesitation,
and with unabated fervor, again shouting "Sieg Heil!" he
stepped forward into empty space, and fell to his death.
As he did, he looked back at me with the telepathic message "Do you understand?" I was deeply mystified.

Remembering Forward

The following night a second episode occurred. It was
of another kind. I seemed to be remembering forward, this
time. War had come, and I appeared to be with some
others in a motor car racing across Poland. The Nazi
blitzkrieg was rolling with enormous power behind us.
The car in which I was being driven was rapidly overtaken
by the irresistible tide of war machines. We were made
prisoner, my possessions confiscated, my books burned. I
then found myself back in Germany in that same Nurem-
berg Stadium, but only momentarily, for it suddenly
metamorphosed into a deep forest glade, with sloping
hillsides. The thousands of people seated in the arena
were now skin-clad warriors, each with his horned helmet
and weapons of battle. I stood, chained to a post at the
open end of this glade among the trees. Suddenly, there
strode forth a powerful figure of a man, who radiated
enormous vitality. Standing near me, he began speaking
forcefully in a gutteral language, shouting to the throng,
and they, in turn responded with what sounded similar to
the "Sieg Heil" that I had heard at Nuremburg. Meanwhile, I was intensely demanding inwardly "Who is he?"
A voice rang within me in no uncertain tones "Alaric,
King of the Goths!" With that revelation, and as though
by signal, the chieftan turned and slew me with his battle
axe. But I now knew who Hitler was.

Awakening from this ordeal undamaged, I could, with
the knowledge of reincarnation, glimpse the pattern of
destiny in Europe as it was about to unfold around Hitler.

I knew that war was inevitable, and it would strike through Poland with lightning speed. But I must learn about Alaric. This was the key to what would happen in the reincarnation pattern.

"Alaric, King of the Goths"

As history tells us, the end of the Roman Empire was marked by Alaric's invasion, and with the sacking of the city of Rome. But the story of how it came about is not so well known.

Alaric, a Visigothic chieftain, was born on the frontiers of the Roman Empire at the mouth of the Danube River, in the region now known as Bulgaria. Although a barbarian, he served in the Imperial Roman Legions that defended this far frontier from the threat of invading Huns from the East. Alaric won his way to leadership under the Emperor Theodosius. He had hoped to become the imperial head of the armies. His dream was nothing less than that of restoring the might of the Roman Empire, which was disintegrating, and he would do it through renewing the conquering power of the Legions. But it was not to be. When Theodosius died, and his sons came to power, Alaric was relegated to a minor office in the local defence. Both he and his fellow Goths rebelled. Alaric was declared 'King of the Goths', whereupon they set out to seek new kingdoms. They unsuccessfully laid seige to Constantinople, then marched westward to Greece, across the plains of Macedonia and Thessaly, pillaging and plundering towns and cities on the way. When they came to Athens, Alaric did a strange thing. It is said that he beheld the goddess Athena Promachos standing on the walls of the city,* and he halted his armies. He sent emissaries into the city, requesting that the greatest poets, philosophers, and musicians be gathered in a central forum where he

*"Byzantium and the Decline of Rome" - W. E. Kaegi, Jr., p. 126 (New York, 1968; Princeton University Press).

could indulge himself in the refreshment of music, art, and stories of the gods. This king of barbarians chose to spend his time in Athens pursuing his odd preoccupation, in addition to receiving ransom, then departed without harming the city of Athens.

Alaric was moody, and had a strong inclination toward the occult. Often he retired alone in the forests to listen to the voices of the gods. Apparently he relied upon these sources for intuitive guidance as to his next objective. Later, after many astonishing adventures, Alaric marched overland to Italy—a march that became a Teutonic migration, bringing wives, children, impedimenta, including captives and the plunder that had been seized. His first attempt at invasion failed, and through treacherous action by Roman ministers, the wives and children that had been taken as hostages were all murdered. This provided Alaric with an additional 30,000 Gothic warriors relentlessly bent upon vengeance. These were the forces that ultimately marched upon Rome and laid seige to the city. The Roman Senate halted the seige through enormous payments of ransom in appeasement. A second seige later resulted in more ransom, and in negotiations which were to place Alaric as commander-in-chief of the Imperial army. But it was too late for that hope. All appeasement failed, and Alaric's army fell upon the city in a third seige that resulted in the sacking of Rome on August 24, 410 A.D., with apparently no great damage done. However, the downfall of the defenseless city marked the end of the "thousand-year rule of Rome". The Goths were Christianized, and the importance of Rome grew in another direction.

Illustrative of reincarnation is the significant denouement of this story, which may have a bearing upon what happened in France in 1940. Alaric continued his victorious conquest of the Italian peninsula. He dreamed of further military expansion across the Mediterranean into

Africa, which was traditionally the food granary of Rome. When the army reached the coast, Alaric ordered his people to build the ships that were needed. His aim now was to bring Africa under his rule. His people labored mightily, with fanatical loyalty and zeal, to obey their heroic leader, whom they idolized.

With the armada of ships ready, they set forth upon this new enterprise. It was an ill-destined venture, for at this point occurred one of those inexplicable natural interferences that have at times altered human history. Hardly had the fleet of vessels cleared the coast, when a sudden storm swept in from the sea, bringing disaster. As the ships one by one were wrecked and sank, they carried to death practically all on board. Alaric escaped with a few of his chieftains, but he had reached the end of his career. His vision and hopes dashed, he died shortly thereafter. A faithful retinue of his remaining people employing a host of slaves, boldly turned aside the flow of a river from its bed, and buried Alaric's body, together with his treasures, beneath the rocks. They then let the stream return to its normal course; and all the slaves were killed. This was done so that none might know what happened to Alaric, or report where his body lay.

Did Alaric Reincarnate as Hitler?

If we view Hitler as Alaric reincarnated, and Rome's reincarnation in Britain, there are strange resemblances between this ancient story and modern history. Hitler and Alaric had the same moody inclinations; they both trusted to intuition; they both sought occult guidance; each dreamed of restoring power to falling Empires. Hitler's secret dream was that of uniting German armed might, with British power and organization, to bring about a 'thousand-year-rule-of-empire'—the greatest the world has ever seen. He sought in several ways to put out feelers toward this end. Was one of them the strange and inexplicable venture of Rudolph Hess's flight to Scotland, at the beginning of the war? Both Alaric and Hitler were instruments that marked the ending of world empires in their time. Both lives ended in spectacular disaster.

Did a Reincarnation Factor Halt the Invasion of England?

When Hitler's blitzkrieg reached the coast of France, there developed a strange display of hesitancy and boastfulness that gave evidence of being a reincarnated group-memory. The miraculous evacuation at Dunkirk had rescued and returned to England the Empire's main body of troops, but they were devoid of arms and equipment of war. England lay prostrate and all but helpless before the threatened onslaught of invasion. The astonishing fact was that the invasion never came about. There are all sorts of strategic and logistic reasons that can be, and were, brought forth to explain the delay at the water's edge, and the termination of the drive westward. Yet there was a singular mystery about the brave stompings up and down the streets of coastal villages and towns in Northern France by Nazi officers, declaring vociferously what they would soon do to England. But the channel was never crossed.

When all this is put together in a frame that includes Alaric's career and final disaster off the coast of Italy, one wonders if there may have been a psychic reason also—a reincarnation factor—that held up the invasion of England. Racial memory could have warned that certain catastrophe would follow any attempt to cross the sea. Was this what really brought to a halt the will to launch an invasion of England? Did a Visigothic memory-bank, awakened by that stretch of water between the coasts of France and England, baffle Hitler's powers, and deflate the German drive westward across the sea?

Another incident that supports the idea of a memory pattern of history repeating itself, was the occupation of Paris. Alaric did not harm Athens, nor did Hitler visit destruction upon Paris, as his air armadas and armies invaded France. Hitler entered Paris with something of a similar respect for the cultural background of Paris, that Alaric had for Athens. It was only at the end, when the collapsing Nazi structure was withdrawing from France, and Hitler, in insane frenzy, knew that his end was approaching, vengefully and futilely ordered the destruction of Paris! It failed. Hitler's Gotterdammerung death and the then current question of his remains, echoed Alaric's end. This general picture illustrates for me, an example of the possibility that nations of people reappear, as such, in the cycles of reincarnation. The old lessons are repeated, as individual souls grow through their trials and errors in the school rooms of national life.

Do Races Remember?

One of the coming changes that will make possible truer histories of mankind, will arrive when historians can take into account the cycles of reincarnation. For one thing, the necessary time-spans will then be provided for placing evolutionary developments in a more reasonable perspective. The enormous spans needed for evolving humanity to its present stage far exceed the lapse of time that modern thought provides. It would require intuitive reasoning indeed, for any attempt to conceive, for example, what the primeval conditions must have been during the first peopling of the Earth. From the point of view of occultism, humanity had not evolved dense physical bodies at that time. For, as we shall see, the reincarnation accounting begins with Life's *involution* into denser stages of matter. The first mankind was ethereal! What then, were natural conditions like? What kind of bodies were these, that human beings possessed? What nourishment was required? What were the animals and trees like? What was man's relationship with Nature? What was the method of procreation, if bodies were not physical? Any investigations into periods so remote may seem to exceed the bounds of sensible enquiry, and to be without any hope of warrantable disclosures. This would be true, except for one fact—memory—both *racial memory*, and the *memory in Nature*.

I am suggesting here that a study of racial memory in the light of reincarnation would reveal a startling diversion from other accounts as to the origin of man. To begin with, we would have to add, as a subtler classification to the present anthropological measurements that distinguish races, and evolutionary stages, *the dimension of racial memory*. For, the conception of reincarnation alters the fundamental bases of observation. Whether we are observing the long-skulled or the round-headed, the woolly or the straight-haired, or the white, yellow, black or brown skin, or other anatomical characteristics, these measurements are themselves the outward features *evolved* from the inward activity of thought, feeling and action native to that people. Further, this inward nature is, itself, shaped by the continuous stream of the play-back of racial memory. The environment of an Eskimo makes demands radically dissimilar to those imposed upon inhabitants of the rain-forests of New Guinea. The necessities of life, and hazards of Nature, have invested the racial group with sharp memories of tragedies and escapes, of triumphs and defeats, of worship and beliefs—all of which stamp the psychic stream with qualities that must parallel in some way the physical measurements classified by anthropology. The 'psychic stream' is the race consciousness, composed principally of group memory, carried unconsciously in every individual member of the race. Faced with similar situations and circumstances, a similar response will be called forth from any member of the race. Individual deviations occur; there are always those who act individually. Presumably such cases are newly reincarnating in that race, or they are withdrawing from it, toward reincarnating in another race altogether.

The Japanese people would offer a very interesting study from the point of view of race memory. Although they are not a distinct race apart from others in South-east Asia, their cultural identity has been so sharply delineated that it suggests a rich and strong racial memory in each individual member. Their legends and myths tell of the people's heroic origins and struggles, and with the coming of their Gods, certain characteristic behavior appeared. The effects of racial memory are prominently displayed in the majority of these people. They must have been re-incarnating repeatedly in the same group to have evolved such decisive delineation of character in a relatively short span of time. The Japanese are not an ancient people.

This tendency to reincarnate in the same race is even more evident in the Jewish people. A study of racial memory in their case, would provide a far richer insight into world development in its fundamental stages in the history of Man. For the roots of these people, according to occult tradition, extend far backward in time to a Semitic people who originated long ago. They were a 'chosen people' from an age incredibly distant in the past, and, whatever conditions they have come under, in many parts of the world, whether scattered in smaller segments, merging with other nationalities, or wandering homeless across boundless lands and deserts, they have remained a people carrying with them a heritage in their racial memory that has had significance in man's past, and will have, in his future.

One of the more amazing factors that emerge from the reincarnational view of world evolution is the measure of time that seems to be necessary to evolve any significant changes in human character. Apparently during certain stages, many millenia elapse with little or no noticeable change in human beings. It is impossible to contemplate this slow evolution without realizing the inequalities in men. For there are unquestionably people in our midst at all times, who seem to change more swiftly; some even, who reach the levels of super-humanity. What it has taken to evolve such great differences in human character and behavior is a profoundly illuminating study.

A "Dreamtime" Humanity

Perhaps the most significant deposit of racial memory on earth today is to be found in the native, original Australians. Of these people the question has been raised by scholars: "Are they the most primitive Race in existence?"* They are not to be classified under any of the main divisions of people, the European, Nordic, Alpine or Mediterranean, the Mongoloid or Negroid, observes Professor Elkin. They seem to be more related to the primitive Caucasian, he thinks, but he has clasified them in a special group as the *Australoid*. Their origin will not be easily educed from their legendary accounts of earlier times, or from their rites, ceremonies, and myths. From these souces come strange revelations of memory that must have been carried in their race consciousness from a past so distant that it is termed, even by their primitive ancestors, "the Dreamtime". This Dreamtime is separated into *The Dreaming* and the *Eternal Dreamtime*. Both of these are sources of communion with the invisible life in Nature, and the non-dying spirit in Man. The dreaming brings knowledge, psychic information and spiritual strength.

Are They Descendants of the First Man?

From their eternal dreamtime have come the mythological stories concerning humanity's origin. These

*"The Australian Aborigines"—Prof. A.P. Elkin, Chapter 1. (Published 1938)

suggest that in the fragmentary records that stretch back into utmost primeval evolution, Man and Nature were much more closely interlinked. How long ago that was, is documented by the plain fact that they record a humanity that existed in a pre-physical or "dreamtime" stage. This seems to imply that their racial memory extends back to a time when mankind had not yet evolved dense physical bodies; they were still in the ethereal stage of descent into physicality! Although such a primeval condition for humanity has no recognition in modern studies of anthropogenesis, this state of evolution does accord with occult records as shown in the geneses of the *Secret Doctrine*,* which tells of earlier times on earth, when humanity had not yet evolved solid physical bodies. Some idea of the distant period set for this pre-physical stage of humanity's evolution is given as somewhere between 10 million and 18 million years ago!** According to the records, Australia was a part of a vast Southern continent at that time, being the habitat of humanity in its ethereal stages. Since Australia apparently did not disappear with the remainder of the land masses, it has had a sheltered existence for an unbroken memory-banking in its humanity, and in its natural flora and fauna, that affords the earliest links we have with the circumstances and origin of Man on this earth.

Perhaps a study of Aboriginal Racial Memory, as evidenced in myths and legends, may establish the Australian Aboriginees as the oldest race on earth, and the direct descendants of the first humanity. With their unmixed race-memory, they may have brought through safely into our times, a great treasure from the past, conveyed in the only enduring measures that man can carry with him throughout the aeons, through all vicissitudes of

*"Secret Doctrine" - Anthropogenesis, H. P. Blavatsky

**Ibid. Volume 3, Ady, Ed. p. 57.

life and death, namely, the immortal treasure of human memory of its past.

Does Nature Remember Infallibly?

The records of occultism inform us that there is a super-sensuous essence that pervades all of Space. It is given the name the *Akasha*. It responds to any and every vibration in the universe, the densest as well as the subtlest, somewhat as sound is recorded on tape. There is no atom or particle of life anywhere that is not recording its surroundings with a 360° lens, photographing in color, sound and subtler effects! This recording that is going on indelibly and permanently in Nature, is known as the *Akashic Records*. It is possible to read the Records.

Psychometry and the Akashic Records

Recognition and appreciation of the memory-banks in Nature has hardly begun. A great deal of exploration and experimentation is needed, even to approach their use. The occult science of psychometry is becoming more widely known. The opening of its fields of investigation has unlimited possibilities.

It is said of Akasha that "it is the Matrix of the Universe . . . from which all that exists is born. . . ."* Cyclically the worlds come forth from rest, as do all other living things in Nature. Their rebirth is a feat of recollection. According to C. W. Leadbeater the Akasha is eternal and it records every tiniest movement of energy. "Each atom retains the record, or perhaps only possesses the power to put the clairvoyant en rapport with the record of all that has ever happened within sight of it" (the substance containing the atom). "It is by means of this quality that psychometry is possible".** The power extends to even

*"The Secret Doctrine" Vol. 4, Adyar Edition, p. 81 - H. P. Blavatsky
**"The Inner Life" - 4th Section. C. W. Leadbeater

thoughts and feelings. It can start from one point as a base and move around in all fields extending from the point. At the disposal of the Adept occultist, this facility would seem to be limitless.

According to this same notable occultist, who has had considerable experience in this region of investigation,

"If one psychometrizes a bit of stone or anything of that sort, all that one can get from it is what one might have seen if one had been standing where that bit of stone was. I have tried, say a pebble out of a valley; it would seem that the pebble has within it somehow recorded everything that has taken place in that valley since the pebble was there, but it does not appear to be able to see over the edge of the valley, or see over the surrounding mountains. The stone itself seems to be able to recall only those things which it has seen and sensed by light reflected from them. But if the psychometrist has got his consciousness into that time and that place, he can then proceed himself to look out over the hills and record what he sees; but the stone itself will never give him that. So, you see, there is a suggestion that light is in some way connected with the matter.

Psychometry indicates getting into touch with some sort of memory. It seems as though everything was impressed by whatever took place within a certain radius of it. It is not a question of distance, but of the straight lines of light. You can recover, through the stone, the arrangement of the stars above the valley, but you can not get half a mile away except by this plan of going back and hunting around on your own account. I think this comes near to proving that there is an association with light in some way. You would see only what the stone could see if your eye was in the stone. If you were a thousand miles away, you would see things a second later than they actually occurred.

We raise our consciousness to a certain level, and are then able to get hold of the Akashic Record—the particular place, country, man we want, and to run it backwards and forwards until we get the point we are after. It is a question whether each of us has a private memory, or whether we have lost the power of getting into touch with that Cosmic Memory.*

There have been explorations by occultists into the primeval history of man. These give evidence of incalculable ages through which our Life Wave of humanity has evolved through cycles of rebirth. Although authentication of evidence obtained in this way remains in fields beyond the reach of modern science and its basic concepts, such horizons are not beyond the powers of reason to grasp and assimilate, if they are viewed from the conceptual position of the involution and evolution of waves of Life through all the kingdoms of Nature. Although the breathtaking, heroic conception of both an involution of life into matter, as well as an evolution of life-consciousness out of matter, is wide open to the wildest imagination, we are preserved from that danger by the rule of reason, logic, and law. Illumined reason is the ultimate protection from delusion; it is based upon clear concepts and a knowledge of the direction in which life is moving. It is possible to gaze sensibly upon the widest horizons, yet to remain within the lawful frame of known truth.

The fact that there are memory banks in Nature, such as the Akashic Records, is no more incredible than the computerized memory banking that is common performance today. If a single case of psychometric investigation—such as the one related above—could be authenticated, the whole of memory-banking in Nature would draw nearer for exploration. These would include memories stored in national and racial consciousness, as well as in world consciousness, and even in that Ultimate Consciousness that created this universe.

With such an awakening of the powers latent in Man, it will be possible in due course, to write the true history of

*"The Inner Life"-2nd Section. Based on a talk given at Sydney, 1923, - C.S. Leadbeater.

the world, and to set straight many a record that has been accepted as true, though based on false or distorted information. Everyone of us, then, is recording life around and within ourselves with *two* sets of memory: the transient memory banks; and the absolute Akashic Records. Brain retention in our transient physical bodies, though it, too, is made up of short term and long term memory storage, is the least accurate of our memory faculties. Immortal memory of the Soul is the least defined, but more long-lasting and influential over greater spans of time. The Akashic memory is perfectly recorded in every particle of our material being, and through any personal articles that may be closely associated with us. Such memory is recoverable, accurately, we may be sure, only by those who have the necessary discipline for the training.

Obviously the mortal recording that takes place in the brain and material bodies, is of no use in recovering memory of past lives, because the material bodies—physical, astral, and mental—do not survive death. Reliable memories of past lives would have to derive from Man's immortal, or *causal body*. This, and the higher bodies are described in the following Chapter.

4

THE ESSENTIAL KNOWING

It is the *knowing*—not the accumulation of knowledge—that illumines with reality the concept of reincarnation. The sum of all that has been known and taught about this doctrine in ancient times, through religions, rites and philosophies, is being looked at upside down by those who in these days insist upon a materialistic point of view on this subject. It is as though today's investigators see only a pot on the fire, analyzing its texture, shape and size, with little attention to what is cooking inside it, and still less to the possible delights that lie beyond the cooking stage. Reincarnation is not a subject to know about. It is known through experiencing, or it is not known. I suggest that we are experiencing it all the time, and failing to recognize the fact, because we are rejecting the idea.

Preparation for Knowing

If we would awaken to what we are experiencing, it would be well to hold lightly any fixed notions we may have about life, death and the hereafter. A flexible mental condition is preparation for grasping intelligently the full cycle of reincarnation, for one must be prepared to move simply and easily upon the way that leads through the mind and beyond, to deeper sources of awareness—a journey from the physical pole of materiality toward its opposite pole.

An early-on experience is the realization that not only does one not die when the physical body dies, the truth is that you *cannot die!* One must be prepared to face that fact, with its implications, which are deep and sobering. The key word in this proposition is "you"—not the pronoun, but the *being*. Who and what are you? This question has been approached in numberless ways, in attempts to unveil the hidden side of man's nature. Although the occult constitution of Man is infinitely complex, it can be contemplated with simple understanding if all essential elements are recognized clearly in their natural order. What, then, is this simple order, the knowing of which, can lead us as by some 'thread of Ariadne' through the labyrinth of endless facts to simply experiencing ourselves as we actually are? Let us see.

First of all, everyone unquestionably knows that he is alive in a physical body. Secondly, there is the certainty that every single physical body dies in time. This transient vehicle is obviously born to die at the end of its cycle. The next thing to know is that when the physical body dies, the *conscious* self that *feels* and *knows* does not cease to exist. How does one know this? By observation.

Awareness in Two Worlds

Certain commonly experienced occurrences will serve for investigation. For example: Have you observed that just before waking from deep sleep—a period when action-dreams and nightmares can happen—that sometimes when the alarm clock goes off you seem to be conscious in *two* realms simultaneously? Two seconds later you are awake and shutting it off, but in that period of two seconds, something happens to time; it expands incredibly;

and you have a long stressful dream that you must run to catch a train that is just arriving, and you find that you are unable to move a leg or foot, no matter how hard you try. Such nightmarish experiences are common. But if you observe them closely, you find that they are actually demonstrations of being conscious in two worlds simultaneously. You are in a non-material world, in a body in which *feeling* is certainly being registered, because you urgently want to catch that train; and you are *mentally* aware, as shown by your knowing you must get on it. But the exasperating situation is that you cannot move the physical body, and you are conscious of it. All of this awareness is taking place in that non-material world, and you are there in some kind of a non-material vehicle to be experiencing it. Yet—and this is the perplexing part—you are sufficiently awake in your physical body to know that you should be able to activate it, but it seems to be paralyzed. Fortunately, in only a moment you are *fully* awake; which really means you pull your selves together in the familiar time-sequence, with integrated inner and outer being, brain and body, that function synchronously when you will yourself to shut off the alarm clock.

The more you think about this experience the more puzzling, yet interesting it becomes—particularly with regard to the significance of the sensation of paralysis. We might compare it with another and more spectacular demonstration of 'two-world consciousness' in which control of the physical body is similarly interrupted.

Appearing in the current news* are reports of hospital patients going through the horrifying experience of waking up on the operating table. According to the report, they find themselves "unable to open their eyes to tell the doctor of their plight because they are paralyzed." It seems that they usually are in great pain, and are terrified; they cannot move or speak, yet are suffering the agony of

*"Sunday Telegraph" - Sydney, October 10, 1976.

physical surgery. These are factual experiences, with case histories sufficiently newsworthy to receive notice in the press.

Obviously, there is a similarity between these cases and the nightmare ones. The paralysis on the operating table seems to be experienced in the same way as the paralysis in the nightmare. The medical explanation of the patient's wakefulness is that some patients are not rendered deeply unconscious with the use of a 'safer' anaesthetic, hence the partial awareness. But this does not explain the psychic, more unpleasant experience of being conscious, yet paralyzed. A knowledge of the occult constitution of man could provide a sensible explanation of what is taking place in both of these instances.

Importance of the "Etheric Double"

What I have said so far, is that everyone is experiencing life through several integrated vehicles simultaneously. Ordinarily this self-system is working efficiently, with the will in control. But when abnormal conditions occur, there is disruption of the information and control mechanisms. Normally, the scene of action is something like this: I know that I am experiencing *feeling* now, in the subtle, non-material emotional body, while at the same time, in another subtler mental vehicle, I am *thinking*. Meanwhile, from the outer world, the physical nervous and glandular systems are receiving impacts, and conveying these impulses and information to the brain, whence they flash through the web of finest physical matter, denoted as 'etheric', into the emotional and mental vehicles, where they are registered as feeling and thought. Responses are instantly flashed back through the system to the brain and physical body, thus motivating action. These impulses are constantly passing back and forth from the dense physical fields through the etheric web to the subtler bodies. This etheric mechanism is of sufficient significance to be designated the *Etheric Double*, because it exactly duplicates the physical body; which means that every physical atom in our bodies merges into its enfolding etheric webbing and thence into the astral matter, thus linking the physical into the astral atom. Throughout our lifetime in the physical body, this 'etheric double' is the conductor of life forces and vitality from higher planes into the physical body. The etheric double is of vital importance to our well-being, and can be readily blocked off, or ejected by anaesthesia. A full anaesthetic therefore produces non-feeling, unconsciousness, because the etheric link with the astral and mental vehicles has been rendered ineffective. A local anaesthetic blocks off a specific area from astral feeling, but does not affect the mental consciousness.

Now, if we think about this etheric-double explanation, and the inter-relationship of our several bodies, from both an objective point of view, and a subjective one, (experienced as meditation), the experiences of both the nightmare, and the operation table instances of simultaneous consciousness in two worlds, appear to be substantiations of the reality that when the physical body is eliminated, feeling and thinking do not cease. For, as we have observed, with a partial absence of the physical body, (shut off by anaesthesia) *self-consciousness continues in the subtler vehicles*. It follows, does it not, that if there is *full* absence of the physical body (shut off by death), self-consciousness will continue in the subtler vehicles. Have we not in these instances, which anyone can experience, a basis for concluding that man's same self-consciousness survives and continues beyond the full elimination of the physical body, i.e. its death?

The Astral Body

Under the term 'astral' there is much information in a number of books that describe the nature and functions of this vehicle. For convenient reference it is only sensible to adopt and retain for this second vehicle of man, the term *Astral Body*. That it quite clearly survives the death of the physical body, is a reasonable conclusion, amply induced by a serious investigation of spiritualistic phenomena. In addition to knowing that I am experiencing life in a physical body, I have no doubt that I am experiencing feelings and desires in the astral body. My nerves and organs are merely transmitters into physical action of what goes on in the astral and mental bodies. This fact conveys a refreshing awareness in me that enables me to abandon the clumsy notion that all of my life happens only in the physical body and brain, and nowhere else.

The Mental Body

It is not too difficult now to realize that enveloping this astral vehicle there is a third, even more subtle one, the *Mental Body*, through which I am experiencing mental life. I must carefully examine just what happens when I think. The burden of knowledge about the mind and all aspects of brain activity is so massive that clearly, the load of learning must be given a new orientation, and trimmed at this point, if we are going to add aspects derived from occultism. Let us not forget that our major aim is to obtain a grasp of the full cycle of reincarnation. In order to do so, we must go on investigating not only the mental function, but searching intuitively beyond the mind, into deeper occult levels of man's nature. A good beginning has been made with the realization that one has a mental body existing entirely apart from the brain. The mental body is a much subtler vehicle than the brain. The question as to which is superior—the brain or the mental body—can be suggestively answered by using an analogy.

If we compare the brain to a computer, then the mental body would be the programmer, or operator of the computer. But there is an owner of the machinery, an overlord director who decides what use will be made of the computer, and this is the *Mind*. The mind uses both the brain and the mental body. The actual thinking is done by the Mind in its vehicle, the mental body. The expression of it in the physical person, is through the dense brain, which acts as a transmitter with computer functions. If the brain is exhausted, the transmission becomes faulty. An injured brain may be unable to transmit the clear thinking that is taking place in the mental body. The physical body and brain wear out, but the mental body does not. The brain grows decrepit, and forgets; while the mental body only grows. The brain may become paralyzed, but this in no way affects the range and resources of the mental body. How often does one grope futilely for words to express what one somehow "knows" somewhere within oneself. This often occurs, yet we must ask, through what instrument do we know that we know something, and cannot express it? The knowledge can be found stored in the mental body.

Once again, at this point, it is a refreshing experience to clear away some of the debris of knowledge that has informed me that the brain is the one and only *knower* within me. If it were, there would be a noticeable difference in hat sizes between a genius and moron.

The Mortal Trinity

But apart from this functioning of the mind, using the mental body and the brain, we have arrived at the awareness that man's personage is actually a triune assemblage of vehicles. His consciousness exists and functions simultaneously in three separate densities of matter—the three worlds of materiality that inter-penetrate without interrupting each other. His physical body, through which he acts, is surrounded and interpenetrated by his astral body, through which he feels; and at that subtler level, the astral body is permeated by his mental vehicle through which he thinks. Intra-body transmission of energies and communication is instantaneous and perfectly integrated. Although three various vehicles are being designated here, one after another, we must not lose sight of the fact that they are all parts of *one* self, just as our limbs, trunk, head and feet are separate parts of one body. The mentioning of parts does not divide and confuse us, or hamper our full free use of the whole body. We are conscious only of *self*—the one user of all the parts. However, as perfect as this functioning can be, the entire trinity is transient, subject to the changes of death. The three vehicles perish in turn during the after-world transition. One can expect that this trinitarian order will be repeated in the several major divisions of Man's being, further on.

Centered Consciousness

The next great realization that changes everything is the awareness of *centered consciousness*. There is a center of *willed* identity—the real Self—from which there is radiation at all three levels—physical, astral and mental—simultaneously. You, the Self, simply shift the focus as you think, feel and act, meanwhile you are centered as an intelligence in all three bodies—and beyond, as well. The centeredness is fundamental. When all three bodies drop away after death, you remain centered in deeper levels. With this realization, one is assured that there can be no death of the individual Self. Certain is the deathlessness of the real *Individual*. As we continue this excursion into Man's subtler nature, centeredness becomes its most significant feature, for it later becomes cosmic centerhood, that merges ultimately in the Absolute Center.

Two Regions of Mental Matter

We will now look again at the mental world to confront a condition that must receive sharpest attention. The levels of mental matter are divided into two regions, each with a distinctly different characteristic. This difference is of fundamental importance in the delineation of Self-consciousness. First, let us consider the 'lower' region of mental matter, from the substance of which is formed the mental body. This body is the vehicle, where all objective thinking and worldly thought takes place. Any use of this mental region of the self results in the creation of mental forms—thought-forms. These thought-forms are naturally attached to their creator. Therefore people surround themselves in this way with broods of mental progency, thus creating their mental world's population and 'atmosphere'. Since the mental content is the direct product of one's life-quality, it is well to realize that the mental world can be recreated by changing the life-quality. The perceiving of the physical world around us, and our intelligent responses to it, is the work of our 'material mind' in the mental body.

The 'non-material mind', on the other hand, functions in the 'higher' region of mental matter which is designated by the term *Manas*. It is of an entirely different nature, being infinitely mobile, flexible, and fluidic. Its activation does not result in congealed thought-forms, rather in radiances that go instantaneously towards any abstract subject that is being contemplated. One uses manas when engaged in non-objective thinking, as in metaphysical speculation. By means of this subtler mind, the truth-seeker may roam the universe, so to speak. But, by this means also, he may set out upon the wildest flights of fantasy. The great difficulty with exercising manas, is that of giving the insights gained through it a practical, useful shape, such as providing a philosophy and faith by which to pattern our lives. Also, it is well to remember that this superior level of the mental self has the power to shape the material mind.

The crucial difference between these two levels of the

mental self is not so much the fact that their characteristics are different, but more importantly, that *they are oriented to opposite poles*. The lower mind is oriented to the material world; it is a part of the mortal trinity; all of its forms perish when life withdraws. The higher manas, on the other hand, is oriented to the imperishable Self within. Manas, in its pure state, is reflective of the Divine Order. Compared with the denser, the subtler mind is a radiant intelligence with limitless potentials. The lower mind is a body generally shaped as we think ourselves to be. The higher mind is formless, but centered in what is termed the *Causal Body*.

Locale of the Reincarnating Self

The causal body does not perish at death, it conveys and transmits the essence of life experiences from one incarnation to the next. It contains the memory-banking of all the past history of the individual, hence it is the repository of one's immortal memory, which includes the sum of causes that one has set in motion in the past, the effects of which are worked out in due time.

We have now taken up our position in the higher manas, departing from the common, daily run-of-mindedness, and have entered the regions used by the great thinkers, the geniuses, and god-like immortals, as well as all the rest of us who do any abstract or universal thinking. No one experiences luminous glimpses of Truth, except through manas. We use manas whenever we are thinking profoundly. There are endless facts to be revealed about this great center of the Self, but the essential one to grasp here is that through manas the *reincarnating Self* is focussed in the causal body.

The causal body is the deep center of immortal consciousness. Through it radiate forces of intelligence from buddhic and atmic levels into mortal man. Through this deeper causal center one begins to experience new dimensions of freedom, realizing that the several centers already mentioned are not merely centers strung together, but are *one* center of consciousness operating in all the levels of the Self. The stepped-up or slowed-down intensities at these various levels are related to the changes in consciousness from a slothful, non-thinking inertia, to mental alertness, and beyond, to inspired genius. It would be much more graphic if one conceived this arrangement of immortal consciousness seated in the causal body as *spherical*. One might perceive the deep center of the Self as radiating through *three* concentric spheres, representing immortal Man's atma, buddhi, manas levels of Self. The immortal Self therefore is conceived as being much more than merely manas seated in the causal body.

The Trinity of Immortal Man

We are ready now to glimpse the higher Selfhood, referred to as the immortal Soul. It consists, as said, not only of manas, but of two other spheres of consciousness mentioned previously. With manas as the basis, the second enveloping aspect of the Soul's trinity is the *Buddhic* sheath. It is characterized by a wondrous love that is all-inclusive, and thus infinitely unitive. In fact, it is this uniting faculty within man's Soul that provides those intuitive illuminations that flash into his mind when he seems to know something from within by becoming united with it through love. This love-intuitive faculty is used when we relate through identifying ourselves with any living thing anywhere. Becoming 'at-one' with it, we know its nature from within. This is made possible by the buddhic quality in matter. The buddhic plane is the fourth of the seven great planes of Nature, the seventh being the physical; the sixth, the astral; and the fifth, the mental. We have to imagine our selfhood in the buddhic world as infinitely adaptable, adjustable and changeable, yet ever centered there in bodiless radiances. Although it may sound unreal and alien, a conscious bodilessness of being is not an uncommon state of awareness. It is experienced, for example, whenever we are absorbed in any abstraction, listening to great music, inspired poetry, or engaged in illumined thinking. One is not aware of the physical body, provided it is normally healthy and comfortable. We use its faculties of seeing, hearing and touching, unconsciously; and so far as the experiencing of the music or the creative thinking is concerned, we are really in a 'bodiless' state of being. Getting used to extensions of this idea of bodilessness can be facilitated by shifting one's attitude from a grasping and holding state of mind, to one of letting go and radiating Reality, as though in consecrated relinquishment of possessions, needing nothing—not even a body. At the buddhic level, consciousness can radiate thus infinitely, in all directions. The extent of this universal expansion outward, which, remember, is inclusive, depends entirely upon the growth and state of unfoldment of the immortal Soul. This is a matter of evolution through the cycles of reincarnation.

The third aspect of the immortal trinity is the Atma—the will center. The deepening significance of centeredness can now be more fully realized. If, in meditation, we should become aware of the buddhic level of consciousness, possibly glimpsing life radiating in all directions, the radiances are necessarily issuing from a central point. That point is not only the buddhic level center, it also deepens into atma, the highest level of the manas-buddhi-atma trinity of the Soul. Atma reflects the cosmic power that is creating the universe. Atma, then, is the will center in the individual Self. Centeredness must now become an all-important realization. With awareness of the atmic center, the wholeness of the Self, mortal and immortal, can be envisioned. But to realize it experientially, we would have to give fullest attention to the purification of our lives, and through knowledge, together with the practice of right meditation, stir the intelligence that is latent in us at these deep levels.

In meditation, the experience of awareness in the higher mental world requires the concentrated focus of attention in the manas center; in the buddhic world it requires harmony with the universal Love that is radiant there; in the atmic world there must be attunement with the power and supreme order reflected there from the Will aspect of life. One can perceive or, rather conceive, the life forces from the mighty Source of All, welling up into the center in the atmic level; thence radiating outwardly as universal love in the buddhic level; and only then reaching manas in the causal body, inspiring the lower self into creative action. This transmission of higher influences can be instituted in meditation, to become inspired and creative thinking that leads to action. Its practice would be the exalted experiencing of the three levels of the higher Self.

The Macrocosmic Trinity

Although we need not go beyond this point to trace a complete cycle of reincarnation, it might be helpful to glance further along, at the third trinity that completes the total Man-God creation. As we have seen, the birth of man's physical body is not the first step in his evolution. Physical evolution began only after incalculable ages of spiritual evolution had taken place in the subtler worlds that precede the physical. The macrocosmic Creation, a universe of Light, came forth initially. This manifestation of God occurred before all else. Then, within this flaming wholeness, the One dissolved into myriads of blazing sparkling centers or individual vortices of fiery forces. These are the radiant centers of sleeping intelligences, destined to become awakened in the vast schemes of evolution that lay far in the future. These sparks in the one flaming Source are called *Monads*—each one is the ultimate source of consciousness deep within every living creature, which includes every human being on this earth. The coming forth of these sparks, or monads, is the second stage of Creation. The monads remain in the primordial substance that fills the universe, and is referred to as the *Akasha*. In it lives forever all that exists. Symbolically speaking, the *One* has now become the *Many*, and during the long course of evolution, the Many re-become the One. The third stage of Creation is the direct projection, by the Logos, of the Archetypal Universe. It exists as an 'embryonic blueprint' of all the worlds, the creatures and the living things that are to be evolved. The monads are attached to the archetypes, and thus appear as perfect beings. Facing outwardly upon the scene of aeonian evolution, each monad becomes the driving force—the 'Father in Heaven' that inspires life ever onward, ever excelling its past achievements in fulfilling the original 'blueprint' for the perfect universe that was projected in the beginning, and shall be wrought in the end.

The Free-Will Factor

Apparently all the time that is needed, has been provided, in which to grow and evolve life's forms and radiances to the perfect archetypal stage. Time is the expandable and collapsible feature that provides the playground of free-will. Evolution can be hurried in individual cases, or delayed, but the achievement of perfection of the whole is certain in the end.

It is a profound spiritual experience to become aware of this existence of an archetypal universe, and thus to realize that archetypes do exist for every creature, every plant and mineral, and that all, including ourselves, are evolving units of life, growing in that direction. This means that it is possible to expose in meditation one's present limitations to the corrective influences radiating from the archetypal Self deep within. Conceivably, one might shorten the duration of one's severest limitations in this way. Perhaps the ailing world can be helped by those who wish to do so and are able through meditation to bring forth showers of archetypal Light into the scene on earth, to illumine the painful path ahead. A knowledge of these profound matters may change everything. But whether we use this knowledge and inner power or not self-perfecting is a cosmic drive that stems from the archetypal world. It urges all living things forever onward whether or not they co-operate. The truly inspired seers and great thinkers who responsibly lead the evolving affairs of the world must somehow be in attunement with the arche-typal 'Plan', to be aware of the right timing for instituting any phases that are currently manifesting.

The Alpha and Omega of Reincarnation

We now have assembled the essential knowledge for viewing in its greatest perspective, the normal cycle of reincarnation as it is being charted here. Man is first of all an imperishable fragment of God. Each fragment evolves an individualized Soul, in accordance with its perfect archetype. The triune Soul is responsible for creating the three transient vehicles of denser matter—mental, astral and physical—in which is experienced life's greatest limi-tation. This pattern serves to awaken the Soul's latent powers. We can understand now, that ages of spiritual beginnings had to precede evolution in the deep and lust-ral seas of matter, the worlds of color and storm. Into this densest matter the mighty rhythm of life dips and ever returns as the evolutionary journey progresses. Immortal man creates, as does the chambered nautilis, his threefold denser garments in ever greater measures of unfoldment. In each incarnation the Self becomes deeply engrossed in the three material bodies. After death the Self is purged of its enthrallment in matter, returning to its immortal base to prepare for another day. It is not until the preceding evolution in the subtler worlds has taken place, that physical man finally arrives upon the scene. Thinking, feeling, creating, growing and dying, he fills out his physical incarnation, and returns to his homeland, the 'country of the Soul', the causal body, which is his center throughout the long series of reincarnations. Blessed is he when he returns each time, bringing a harvest of love and good service; woe, if the burden is of selfishness and hate. But, whatever the vicissitudes, he remains the immortal Self, unborn, undying, ever unfolding. Thus may be perceived the primordial meaning of Life spread upon the boundless universe.

Let us summarize in a rapid glance, the journey of an incarnation. It *begins* in the causal body. The new cycle opens with the Soul's knowing of the past and the goals that lie ahead, and thus prepared, being drawn into the descent when the mental and astral 'permanent atoms' are activated. Magnetically linked to these are all the atoms of the old-new mental and astral bodies. These will reproduce exactly the capabilities and limitations that have been evolved so far. Nothing has been lost. Every attainment is retained forever, but some of the qualities developed in the past may remain latent, unawakened in any particular life. The mental and emotional environments, which include parentage, race, and country, are determined by the forces of karma, and are inherited accordingly.

Finally, the whole reincarnating structure is seated in the physical body that now comes to birth in its mother's womb. The formation of the physical body is entirely regulated by the dispensations of karma, and the immediate destiny of the Soul. Here is the arena for the vivid play of *memory*. The foetus 'remembers' the physical past evolution from mineral, to vegetable, to animal. The newborn infant begins recovery of his evolutionary emotional and mental past, the primeval fears and innocent delights, the savage aggrandisements and atavisms of primitive man, as well as the glories of untutored wonder. The normal child recalls Soul-memories of love and idealism; the youth 'remembers' his talents and past achievements in choosing his life's course; the adult—remembering at a deeper level—opens new wells of power and knowledge amidst the struggles of life; the aged begin to 'remember' the realities beyond physical life.

The return journey inward, after departure from the physical body, is simply a procedure of dissociation from the entanglements with materiality at each level, the etheric, the astral and mental. The heaven-world requires a far longer period of time for this purpose but heaven, too, finally concludes in the return of the Soul to the splendor of its imperishable Selfhood. Only then, does the normal cycle of an incarnation reach its closing period in complete refreshment and renewal. All is well then with the Individual as he awaits once more the action of the great rhythmic forces of Life to sweep the Self downward into new conditions of change and great challenge, of bondage and confinements, the overcoming of which, in a life well-lived, advances the Soul along its individual way to Archetypal Perfection.

Such is the essential knowing of the cosmic rhythm of reincarnation.

5

TRIUNE ENLIGHTENMENT

We must now consider further the principle of balance in the universe. It is functioning everywhere, in everything around us, in the worlds, the heavens, and in every positive-negative orbit of forces that constitute the atoms. Nowhere is there anything in motion, or in equilibrium, that is not under the aegis of this super-principle. It extends its rule into the very thoughts and feelings that motivate the action of our daily lives. Each exertion of energies produces its chain of action and reaction, each cause generates its return to equilibrium. From the beginning of time, and throughout the evolution of the universe, in endless cycles within cycles, this eternal principle has operated ceaselessly. It underlies chaos, yet is the very foundation of ordered cosmos. It rules man's creation himself, and rules as well the fiery explosions of new-born stars, and their growth to giant fullness, their decay and ultimate collapse into neutron-death in the black-hole graveyards of space; yes, and this law will govern the rebirth of universes in an unimaginable future. Such is the sway of the Law of Karma.

The day I awakened to this principle, which until then was unknown to me, I walked forth to new freedom within. Humanity's agonizing cries of *Why—Why does this happen to me?-Why are some people born to endless blessings, and others to unending pain and sorrow?— Why so much injustice?*—All such questions that had held me in their paralyzing grip for so long, were transformed now into *How. How does this law operate? How does this principle function? How do we live harmoniously within this ceaseless chain of action and its return to balance?* Cause and consequence, like waves in the sea, follow each other incessantly. If we could grasp the dynamics of these mysterious rhythms, not only would a great light be thrown upon the purpose of life, but upon the mastery of those forces that limit life's expression in us. We would grasp more clearly the wonder and the seriousness of our human situation—perceive meaning in the tragedies that go unexplained.

I saw a man working beside me on a building construction job fall to his death because he missed his step on a narrow plank. But, was that simple fact the *only* cause of such a calamity to his family? Death struck without warning, and apparently without reason or purpose other than the physical mis-step. On the other hand, I myself experienced a life saved, just as casually and apparently as meaninglessly. A derrick that was lifting steel to the top of a building, cracked, and its load crashed exactly where I had been standing for hours giving signals to the operator. But at that very moment, for no reason at all, I had walked fifty feet away. Why? Was it only random chance that determined these two contrasting events—a life lost, a life saved? Or did they occur under some rule of universal law?

Without knowledge of karma, the casualness of so-called 'fate' baffles the mind concerned with truth. In an accident involving many persons, death seems to strike capriciously. On a huge construction job I saw the disastrous parting of cables strung from towers high in the air, that were holding heavy iron chutes down which streams of concrete were pouring to the foundations of a building, and witnessed with horror the chutes fall upon workmen below. In the resulting havoc, this man and that one died instantly, others were hurt, yet there were men standing in the midst of the crashing metal and cables who remained untouched. Was this a scene of aimless luck, good and bad? These, and similar incidents deepened my perplexity. My efforts became more intense, to discern why such things are happening every day. I could not believe that *all* is random chance, despite appearances.

Surely, it was not simply chance that determined what happened to the air hostess who, according to press reports, was in the tail of a great air-liner when it exploded at high altitude, killing everyone except herself. In addition to this incredible fact, the tail of the plane broke away and fell 30,000 feet, to strike the granite precipice of a mountain peak, and slide down snowbanks into the forest far below. When the hostesss was found, she was not only alive, but not desperately hurt. Some force superior to the normal laws of Nature governed that descent of a frail human body—some absolute destiny that over-rides all else, prevailed. What super-principle governs all laws of Nature?

The Law of Karma

As has been said, motion is seeking universally a return to balance. At every level—whether it be physical, emotional or mental, or even higher spiritual levels—no force can be generated that does not inevitably return to equilibrium. The entire cosmic process might be summed up as a primal upset from an original state of equipoise, into cycles within cycles of infinite motion that ultimately returns the whole system to equilibrium and rest. The law is inviolable. When a ball is thrown into the air, it falls back to earth and doesn't stop rolling until all forces are equilibrized. The principle of karma can be expressed as simply as that. But its application extends to all planes of the universe in terms of energy and force. This lawful motion was recognized in the past, and expressed in various terms having the meaning that karma has today. Religious creeds and beliefs have given it cognizance, particularly in the fields of morality. Its recognition lies behind many admonitions that were more understandable and practiable when reincarnation was known generally by the people of the world. One understood that sooner or later, in this life or the next, one would meet just compensation for all acts committed or omitted.

Karma and Reincarnation

With the rise of Western civilization, poised upon a single creed, a single God, and a forgotten past, the law of reincarnation disappeared from mankind's schooling, and the fear of death became predominant. Without multiple lifetimes to inherit the results of what is sown, the idea of karma loses its true meaning. As reincarnation's great light passed into obscuration, karma could be, and was, relegated to the ranks of alien superstition. "God's will" sufficed as explanation for, "Why does this happen to me?" But this outlook does not encourage the spiritual sense of responsibility and self-confidence that would be the case if we were taught an enlightened comprehension of the principle that neither rewards nor punishes, but simply balances all action with its exact effect, present and remote—whether in this lifetime, or the next.

Knowledge of this law's dependability can be used as surely in adjusting life's situations, as the law of gravitation is used in the construction of buildings. But if through ignorance the law is transgressed, the result will be painful, whatever the good intentions might have been.

Karma as Corrective Feedback

Karma can be viewed in a number of ways, and described in terms suitable to any student. In a mechanistic reference, for example, one might interpret karma as a kind of universal "feed-back" system that is automatically rectifying the inefficient and disharmonious use of our machinery of existence. If we are clumsy and thoughtless in the handling of machinery, we not only damage it, but will soon lose the use of it. If I misuse my physical body, it is only common-sense to recognize that the forces that I have set in motion will flow back upon me, and since they are destructive, they will tend to wreck my body. But if I live carefully, thoughtfully, helpfully, in all three of my bodies—physical, astral and mental—the forces engendered will react beneficially, assisting my course through life.

In fact, these forces might be compared to the air currents that aid the flight of an eagle, or sea bird. I once stood at the stern of an ocean liner that was crossing the Tasman Sea, watching the tireless flight of an albatross as it followed the ship, day in and day out. The bird seemed to exert no visible effort in its flight. It soared ceaselessly, with apparent ease, floating higher in the air, then dipping down and skimming the waves to the right and the left, never passing the ship, but ever following behind. How could any muscle tissue respond inexhaustibly to such unremitting demands? How can an albatross be so tireless? Watching it, I realized that it was balancing with extraordinary skill, the air currents and the forces of gravity, by the slightest manipulations of feathers and wings. The albatross was *gaining* strength while flying! There is a revelation in this demonstration of consummate art in using the forces of life. Why cannot human beings, too, live with that supreme art in their worlds of forces and energies? Once we recognize the universal principles that are continuously employed in all our actions, we might manage a harmonizing alignment of all forces. Knowing and utilizing these principles might help us, with greater ease, to balance the demands of our environment and pressures of daily life with the drives of our emotions, desires and thoughts, as well as any elevating spiritual currents that we are channeling. Such a skill could restore energy through harmony, instead of wasting it in conflict. Thus, one might live out one's incarnation more skillfully and purposefully with the energies that are available.

Man, being a self-generator of innumerable thought-patterns and desire-impulses, each of which becomes a circuit of forces that automatically includes the reaction that has been generated, must see to it that these karmic circuits become less painful, limiting and harmful. How mistakenly we use energies, struggling to close every door against adversity, rather than expending the same energies to meet life everywhere creatively. We cannot normally forsee karma, nor block it, when it arrives; it will materialize out of the very walls of success, to harass us with fresh concerns. On the other hand, we can modify its effect through discriminative perception, greater awareness and wiser attitudes. We need not be daunted when confronted with perilous and seemingly impossible odds. Sometimes the miraculous does take place, if it is 'in our karma'. During the first World War, when the ocean liner *Lusitania* was sunk by a torpedo, there was a man aboard dying of pneumonia. He went into the icy sea with everyone else, and was not only rescued, but found to be recovered from his pneumonia. When the forces of karma from the past rule otherwise, destiny makes impossible one's death before its appointed hour.

In the foregoing chapter we gained a basic knowledge of man's nature, as comprehended from the point of view of occultism. With that knowledge, we are in a position to observe more precisely how the law of karma works. There are three main streams of karmic forces operating in our lives. They are, first, *Pending* karma, the forces of action and reaction that are created and discharged currently in this lifetime. Secondly, there is *Stored* karma, that is carried over from the past, and may or may not be discharged in the present life. Thirdly, there is a large-scale, *Collective* karma that links a person to larger family, national, racial, and world groups that create karma, and inherit together the consequences.

Pending Karma

This first category of karmic action is readily observable in ourselves and others. Who isn't aware that if he foolishly indulges his appetite for rich food, or anything else, he will 'pay the price' as the saying goes. Again, if one carelessly walks off the edge of some high place—even though one's thoughts may be at the loftiest elevation—the physical body will nevertheless be subjected to the law of gravitation in some painful way. Similarly, all excessive indulgences invite painful results. In this connection, 'sow the wind, and reap the whirlwind' is the oft-quoted allusion. The quotation is familiar to us because there are so many examples of it around us. Cruelty inflicted on others earns the worst form of infliction upon ourselves. Karmically speaking, both the sowing and the reaping must be seen as a single action; they are the action-reaction cycle of karma. We strike, and are struck down, we strike back—this can go on, ad infinitum. What is the intelligent action?

Stored-Up Karma

More obscure is this type of karma. But, for those with a knowledge of reincarnation, its nature is recognizable as delayed cycles awaiting equilibration. The span of time between the causal action and the returned reaction may have stretched across lifetimes, despite which the hour inexorably arrives when a balance will be struck. One does not remember what it was that took place in a past lifetime that brings in this life some apparently unearned calamity, or, on a happier note, some bonanza that arrives seemingly without cause. Usually, mortal man knows only the bewildering, inexplicable 'bolt from the blue' that strikes him. This kind of karma is much harder to bear, and is apt to stir resentment against life's apparent injustice. It may blight one's attitude toward learning the deeper lessons that are to be perceived in all adversity. In extreme cases a knowledge of karma's law not only may restore one's equilibrium, but may even rescue one's sanity. In the modern confluence of dire necessities, with the demand for satisfactory explanations, it appears to me that the dereliction of serious interest in the twin laws of karma and reincarnation may be seen as the most striking deprivation in twentieth century culture.

It would be of enormous assistance to know instinctively that our mortal lives are spent in the schoolrooms of racial, national, and cultural patterns imposed, in which the non-dying Self, sprung from no race or nation or breed—nor with loyalties to any—is developing his own superior potentials while remaining firmly cemented in the cosmic structure of the whole. Were this the prevalent teaching, there would be but few who are unable to understand more clearly what is expected of all of us as human beings, and to co-operate more fully with the advantages that would be offered in a world-wide fraternity of modern life.

There are times when the immortal Soul is barred from further progress because of karma incurred in the far past. When the time arrives for balancing the scales, the barricade will be removed. Yet it seems that in severe cases there has to have been developed the strength to bear the worst before the event does arrive. There is, therefore, a 'right time' in which one meets the larger karmic events. Happy is the individual who is ready with a knowledge of life's laws to adjust to whatever comes.

My accident that was related in the opening chapter in this book, is a case in point. Through no apparent fault of mine, I was struck down, and my body made to suffer crippling effects for life. For many years, prior to the event, I had devoted my full energies to serving the cause of beauty and human enlightenment. Seemingly I had set in motion no forces in this life, at least, for such a blow to strike me. Had I been ignorant of life's laws at the time of that accident, I might have become embittered by it. But the right time had come, I was prepared with knowledge; so I was able to experience the blow with no resentment, in fact, no feelings against anything—even against the man who struck me down. It was not he who damaged me, but I who generated the cause in some forgotten episode of another lifetime. In the larger, immortal perspectives, Life's laws were actually working beneficently, that the interior Self might progress onwards. The enduring effect of the accident was that of deepened illumination and greater capacity to serve with vision.

The working out of *Stored* karma offers another opportunity for the appearance of memory from the past. The closing of these weightier cycles are themselves a form of memory. A common manifestation of this type of memory is the cautioning that one receives through that inner prompting that we term 'conscience'. While in the midst of action, conscience warns us to avoid repeating some misstep that resulted in sorrowful experience in the past. The voice of conscience is a 'recall'. This playback of karma comes as a stirring of Soul-memory. Conscience is the bell tolling a warning that we have suffered shipwrecks in the past, on the very reef we are approaching again. The nearer we are to fully awakened Soul-memory, the greater will be our alertness to the voice of conscience.

Collective Karma

The reincarnationist views life as essentially spiritual, because it is in that greater reality of the ultimate Self that the imperishable spark—the monad—exists, dwelling within the One Life. Terrestrial life, due to its changeability and brevity, must be considered as illusory. Hence the karma of the greater cycles, the path of the monad in the vast orbit of spiritual evolution, the ray he is upon, the series of lifetimes it takes to awaken his divine potentials, the racial and national bonds he will establish, the larger communal and family groupings with whom he evolves through long ages of time—all, are creating 'group-karma'. This more extensive bondage is included under the heading *Collective* karma. National disasters and racial persecutions are examples of this kind of karma working out. A nation of individuals acting as a group, who perpetrate cruel and unjust acts, earns stored up collective karma that will be released through the sufferings of the returned group of individuals. Families often evolve together through long series of lives, earning and receiving collective karma.

Nationalities that have evolved and maintained special human traits and capacities through great spans of time, apparently do so through individual members in greater numbers, reincarnating together repeatedly. Strong karmic ties bind them in their specialized developments. Sometimes extraordinary Souls who have evolved far ahead of their people, reincarnate among them to guide and teach them. Such an example is seen in the great Booker T. Washington, who served faithfully the welfare of his race in the U.S.A. He was the son of a former slave in America, who brought untold advantages to his people. Great leaders come as beneficent collective karma, returning good for the selfless service rendered by the whole group. Conversely, a nation, through failure to serve its manifest national destiny, will draw forth leaders who betray it, and who will lead to its downfall. There is no lock on God's 'back-door' of reincarnation. All of us are unavoidably involved in group cycles of collective karma—family, national, and world karma. Therefore, the larger the civic and community services that we are able to render, the greater are our opportunities to earn for the group, as well as for ourselves, a more splendid future of larger opportunities for spiritual unfoldment.

Karma works with the same exactitude in global catastrophies as it does in the delightful balance of forces that unveil a rainbow in the sky. Sir Rabindranath Tagore, a great poet who was also a master of life, could say with equanimity: "Clouds come floating into my life from other days, no longer to shed rain, or usher storm, but to give colour to my sunset sky." Of all the advantages offered by a growing understanding of the law of karma, the most rewarding is the change it can bring in our attitude toward everyone around us, and to all events of life, good or ill. If one's situation becomes unfortunate and threatening, it is not to prayers and penitence that one must turn in the self-made prison, but to action employing the law. Deliverance begins from within; the powers are there, enticed forth by the circumstances of life as these rise about us.

Dharma

But the greater enlightenment that the knowledge of reincarnation and karma brings, depends upon a third law that must be equated with reincarnation and karma. Reincarnation occurs not only because of stored-up karma that must be worked out, but also because of the evolutionary aim of life's perfection. Both reincarnation and karma serve this higher principle that urges ultimate Perfection. The ceaseless attraction in that direction may be designated as a law of *Spiritual Evolution*. It imposes the need for a subtler discrimination between what is lawful and unlawful action, between morality and immorality. "Mysterious is the path of action", stated Krishna in the Bhagavad Gita (4:16-17). It is so because current ideas of morality and man-made laws are ever superseded by a higher morality that has its basis in universal laws that govern the Divine Self in man. In the Buddhist canon, this is the sacred law of *Dharma,* or spiritual duty, as distinguished from all other worldly duties. Dharma is not an outer law, or absolute path of righteousness that is the same for all. It is a commandment of the unfolding inner life of the individual that necessarily must tend to mould his outside environment and events to expressions of himself. Each individual has his own dharma, his true inner destiny, his spiritual necessity. It acts as the law of his *next stage* of unfolding. Dharma is of the future. It is the forecast pattern of what is to be unfolded, just as karma is an after-cast pattern of the past. Together, the two are the unfolding *past-future pattern,* that is ever aligned, in a direct path, with the evolutionary goal of perfection.

These three laws: reincarnation, karma and dharma, viewed simultaneously, become an interwoven 'triune enlightenment'. They cannot be truly conceived singly, apart from one another. Together, they underlie all that is happening. Mortal man, in his mundane life, is confined in the structures of *pending karma*. Meanwhile, his immortal Self is holding him steadily upon the way of *dharma* to freedom. Overshadowing both is the Divine Man, the heavenly parent, shining as a star apart, pointing the true way of balancing the larger measure of *collective karma* with the dharma of the individual—the action that leads him to final liberation.

6

DEATH—FICTION AND FACT

With the glimpse we have had of life's basic rhythms and laws, attention can now be turned to a closer inspection of the mysterious doorway of death that opens the transcendental journey inwardly to completion of an incarnation.

The Great Delusion

Nowhere do we encounter sharper differences of outlook and ideas, than in our concern with what happens to us when we die. In this direction, today's dependence upon science and technology for answers to man's ultimate physical problem, his death, comes to an abrupt stop with the last expiring breath of the body. And those who limit their beliefs about our fate at the end of life to ideas founded upon material science, are apt to follow its tacit conclusion that there is no life after the death of the body. Others, who must have a faith that they can live by, and die with, resort to religion and philosophy for their personal convictions. There are rarer individuals, so vital with life, that for them, there can be no thought of death; they seem to be free of any fears about it. And finally, there are the few who know instinctively that life is far grander, richer, and more wondrous than the sorry tale of mortality being depicted for us by the majority of materialistic modern thought.

The greatest teachers of mankind have ever looked compassionately at the world about them, seeing the burden of sorrow, suffering and death, and have sought to alleviate man's plight by revealing truths that stand behind the illusory world. It is in this tradition that a knowledge of reincarnation is used here to confront some of the fictions about death that are current in our day.

The central fact to be faced is the finality of the death scene. A person is living one moment, and the next he is gone beyond recall. Is this the end of his intelligence, the writing off of all his accumulated knowledge, his developed vision, the hopes, the dreams? It is the argument of this book that Man does not die—indeed, that he is an imperishable being.

More Intensely Alive

But even if the proposition that we cannot die is adopted as a basic fact, there still remains the great sorrow that descends upon anyone who experiences the death of a dear friend or beloved relation. The finality of separation forever is a traumatic shock that might be alleviated if there were available some clear accounting, some acceptable and guiding information about what happens on the other side; and how one fares in those invisible worlds. There can be relief from anxieties and grief with the knowledge that is available about life's continuance beyond the death of the physical body.

It is not easy to understand the fine points of a game of chess if one knows only the names of the chess pieces. Even more difficult is it to explain the game of life beyond the physical realm, when the nature and powers of the bodies and principles of man are names only, and not

78

recalled experientially. The simplest way to enquire into the strange mystery of death, is to begin with the familiar experience of living. When one is riding horseback, or sailing a boat, dancing, or listening to music, the essential experience in each case, is the *state of consciousness* that is induced by these activities. This induced awareness is actually the experience of being alive in those ways. Two people in love communing together, are sharing a vivid experience, but it is the state of awareness, rather than the physical presence, that is the living experience. This distinction between registering physical impacts, and experiencing the state of consciousness that arises from them, is the essential understanding to be grasped in realizing the continuity of life beyond the physical plane.

Anyone who is deeply appreciative of music and immensely enjoys listening to it, knows that it is not the vibration of the ear-drum that is appreciated; it is the quality of consciousness evoked by the impacts striking the ear drum. It may seem an odd idea, but I believe it to be true, that were anyone to die suddenly while listening to splendid music, his consciousness of the music would be instantly enhanced beyond any capacity of hearing it through physical ears alone.

I think this is illustrated whenever someone who is doing creative work, uses a stimulant to overcome the lethargy of the physical self. The nerves and brain are rendered somewhat more functional in transmitting the intensity of the inner life that is ever shining more vividly beyond the physical veil. This means that the vibratory capacity of the physical body can be stepped up, and more of the inner life may be transmitted. Clearly, the inner life is more vivid than that which is in the heavy physical body. But dependence upon the use of stimulants to intensify this transmission of moreness, is not the true way to channel it. The reliable and durable method that is as old as time, is simply to discipline and train the bodies to greater sensitivity and refinement.

So, the first fact to realize is that life beyond death is an *intensification* of consciousness. The essential quality of life continues without physical expression. Therefore we can dispose of one fiction about death: that when the body dies, 'there is nothing beyond'. The fact is that when the body dies, the Self is more intensely alive.

Into Freer Motion

The fact that death of the physical body leaves one more intensely alive, may be grasped in another way if we realize that the most exciting feature about being alive is the experience of motion.

Life is movement, alternation, extension; it is the adventuring physically into new and interesting places, new environments, seeing new faces, thinking new ideas; it is the change from action to repose; from negative to positive influences; it is the experiencing of rhythmic dissimilarities; from light to darkness to light; it is even the shifting of things about in one's daily routine. Next to this vivid awareness of movement and motion, is *anticipation* of motion—the excitement of a hoped-for journey, the looking forward to changes in environment and relationship—all of those excitements that are the anticipation of additional movement. The fiction that death of the physical body is the end of motion, is denied by the fact that in the physical body, awareness of motion *intensifies* as consciousness is elevated to higher stages of being; for example, from laboring in the factory to listening to music. On earth, one can see that turgid passion is a slowed-down state of consciousness, by comparison with that of the inspired thinker; while the most inspired thinking does not reach the intensity of pure spiritual illumination, which itself becomes immensely stepped-up in a state of cosmic-consciousness. At that highest level, we may expect to find that God-consciousness is the most intensified motion in the universe, because He is said to be *omnipresent*, which means being everywhere at the same time, the vibratory intensity of absolute abstract motion.

It becomes a matter of simple reasoning to replace the fiction that death ends all motion, with the fact that consciousness released from the heavy physical body, is in a state of freer motion. Consequently, if the quality of life-consciousness is equated in terms of vibratory intensity, or movement, we can dispose of another fiction about death: that all movement ceases when the body dies. Movement of consciousness increases as its vehicles become more subtle. During the transition that takes place when death occurs, the quality of consciousness changes. Its intensity doesn't diminish; it grows, it opens out. This is the actual fact in untold millions of normal cases of physical death. There are numberless abnormal cases too, which will have special attention given them later.

The "Remains"

Another fiction about death is the notion that a deceased person must continue to have some kind of a link with his physical remains. Of course, the sentiment is true and beautiful that we want to render the last loving care of someone dear to us, but the superstition is cultivated that the physical body must be preserved at any cost. Yet we face the indubitable fact that the physical body's extinction is final and complete. The more quickly the departed one can be separated utterly and forever from it, the better. It is preferable to dispatch the remains more rapidly, such as through cremation. It might be even more satisfactory in the light of Reality to dispose of the physical remains by instantaneous atomization. The fact is that undue efforts to preserve intact the form, is a disservice to the departed person, who needs to continue progressing inwardly, and should not be retarded in his progress by the magnetism issuing from the corpse and cemetery influences of sorrow, grief and hopeless sentiments. These

81

links attract him again to materiality. The longing to cling to a physical form, and to maintain it unchanged, is as futile as clinging to some childhood toy. The living consciousness moves onward, and all true relationships move with it deathlessly.

Probably the dread that many people feel about death is largely due to a natural shrinking from the unknown, from any omnious change that might turn out to be to one's detriment. People readily believe that the changes that accompany death are likely to loom unhappily for them. This is largely due to the kind of warnings they have heard about what is "over there". An opposite viewpoint could as readily be engendered in everyone. If, having heard from childhood the story, that life is a universally ongoing growth into greater wonder—an immortal process of unfoldment in this world, and the next—if this view had prevailed in our schooling, and had been reiterated in our mature years, there would be little or no fear of death to plague us.

Heaven is Unique

Another fiction that could be happily eliminated from one's general understanding, is that the after-life is somehow reduced to a lowest common denominator, and that everything is standardized everywhere at that level. A century ago, the fiction generally spread about in Western cultures was a materialized image of heaven—a place of ostentatious wealth and rest. The streets of heaven were said to be "paved with gold", and the dead to inherit wings and harps, and to be generally preoccupied with doing just about nothing. This scene, vividly described, was offered as the "heavenly reward" for a virtuous life. Heaven was thus set forth as a standardized monotony. The truth is that just as every person living on earth is unique, so in worlds beyond the physical, each individual continues to be unique, each finds his individual path of return to God. If we do not use imagination and supreme intelligence in trying to conceive of consciousness beyond us at any point, we resort to a form of inertial mentality that has led to the more absurd notions and superstitions. This fault has given rise to the fiction that some kind of metamorphosis into a divine indolence occurs when man's consciousness departs finally from the physical brain and body. The fact is that consciousness continues forever unfolding uniquely, with or without the limitation of the physical vehicle.

Moments Before and After Death

There are numerous fictions about the experience of approaching death, and the state of consciousness that immediately follows. It is commonly noted that in deaths through fatal disease and old age, a natural point is reached in the terminal stages when the will to live ceases. Generally, dying people realize it when the pendulum of life has swung to another orientation. From that moment onward, the person knows that he is dying; and he accepts it, realizing that he will no longer be able to experience vital consciousness through his deteriorating physical body. This change in orientation, is often accompanied by an extraordinary atmosphere of peace and benevolence, of confessions and forgiveness, and of visions of loved relatives and friends who have previously passed away. The fiction that is generally propagated is that such visions are hallucinations of the weakening mind. But the fact is that this awareness is clairvoyant perception in the astral body, being received through the etheric double into the deteriorating brain, and made possible by the weakening resistance of the materialistic physical brain.

A renowned Chicago psychiatrist, Dr. Elisabeth Kubler-Ross, said recently: "I was curious about what happens when a person dies, one moment I would be holding hands and talking with the patient. . . the next moment I

would be holding hands with a corpse. The person had left. But there were generally most peaceful expressions on their faces, and I wanted to know what caused these."*
Dr. Kubler-Ross also mentioned the phenomena of "hallucinatory stages" that some patients entered into just before they died. But these are not experiences of hallucination, they are psychic perceptions of something that is beyond the physical senses, and often accompany this shift in consciousness when there is realization that one is dying. The focus of awareness has changed from the brain center, to its new center outside the physical apparatus.

The aforementioned psychiatrist reported that some patients described death as a 'floating sensation', a general 'disembodied experience', during which they occasionally saw themselves in the room in which they had later died, being resuscitated by their own doctors. One woman describing the fantastic peace and wholeness that she felt, wanted to tell those fighting for her life to 'relax and let her go'. Her experience is one instance among innumerable others of those who die in homes and hospitals, quietly making the changeover by letting go the physical body and the scenes of this earth.

A Change of Focus

Death is no great change after all, so far as consciousness is concerned. The change in focus might be compared with enjoying the mixed physical and higher sensations of eating a hearty meal while watching an absorbing program on television; then upon finishing the meal, continuing to look at television with full concentrated awareness focussed upon what it is communicating. Consciousness was first aware in two states: that of the physical satisfactions; and that of the visual mental-emotional state. When it shifted, it was a change from a visceral to a

*"Sunday Telegraph" - Sydney, June 15th, 1975.

84

visual awareness. The shift in consciousness was simply a refocussing of attention at a higher level of being. This is precisely the same kind of shift in consciousness that takes place at death. The individual simply experiences consciousness shifting to another level. One might compare dying with going to sleep after a hard, wearying day, and waking the next morning, after a full night's rest, in bright sunshine, with eager anticipation of the new day's activities. The difference being that the waking will not be morning on earth, but new life in the astral world. When the body is young and healthy and without fear of pain, each day's experience is a glorious adventure. So is death's adventure, when the weary physical body with its suffering, is left behind, and one awakens in the tireless astral body. The weariness felt in the dying physical body is not experienced in the immortal Self. The fact is that the Self is exuberantly fresh when there is freedom from the physical body.

Art of Dying

Any anxiety about dying results in a rigidity, of not 'letting go', in clutching and clinging to what should be dropped. If there can be an easy state of mind about releasing one's hold on material things, as though in taking flight, it will be found that one simply falls asleep for a period of hours, or days, before awakening in 'one's place' in the astral world. Departure from any level of life is not forever. We always return to what we were doing until we are through doing it, because what we were doing at any time or place, is some part of the Soul's unfoldment of its full potentials. It is only with the full stature of its growth attained through many reincarnations that there is final departure for the Soul from physical limitations. Meanwhile, the awareness of consciously growing, is a state of happiness; just as, in order to be happy, one needs the sense of growing. Since growth is an eternal state for the Soul, the prospect of happiness is infinite for every human being. It is a fiction to believe that sorrow and gloom are inevitable concomitants of death; rather, death is another blossoming for the Soul; it is a doorway opening outward to life and liberation and therefore to be greeted with joy. Such an outlook would provide the basis for dying gracefully, beautifully, and with dignity. I attended the death of a great Theosophist, who passed on in this manner: he died happily, even jovially, though in pain, knowing what lay ahead and to what his dharma would call him.

Since today's science and technology have progressed in their researches beyond the denser physical fields, one might hope for development of a deeper 'science' of death based upon knowledge of the occult world. The relatively new field of Thanatology seems to be moving in this direction. Although a comparatively new approach, Thanatology offers help, not only to the terminally ill, but to families that survive such patients.

Many terminal cases receive painfully inadequate attention in this respect. A person who is in the terminal stage of a disease passes through the various psychological stages before he reaches mental reconciliation with his fate. During this period of 'descent into darkness' it would be helpful, in most cases, if there were someone trained in Thanatology who could explain the naturalness of this passage through death, rendering it as factual and beautiful as it truly can be when there are no fears or other emotional disturbances to distract the dying from full attention to their finest hour. And such it can be, if death can be shown as offering the greatest opportunity in one's life to achieve extraordinary heights of illumination. Out of a technical knowledge, an art could develop, one of the high arts of civilization: the art of dying beautifully, peacefully and instructively, as demonstrated by Socrates at his death. No one has a finer opportunity afforded him in which to convey to his friends and loved people, such a gift of unforgettable exaltation and enlightenment, as he has at the time of his departure from this physical realm. For those who understand the cycles of reincarnation and know to what levels they return between physical incarnations, this esoteric knowledge is even more helpful than the outer, psychological knowledge and acceptance of the act of dying.

The Earth-Bound

Those who die, yet remain there clinging, in the transition condition that immediately follows death, are referred to as "earth-bound". This is not a normal condition—yet there are many who, due to various causes, such as trying to clutch to physical materiality, or their previous indulgences in vices, and greed; and among them, those whose violences led to their death, remain in a continued conscious attachment to the world scene. These people have not awakened in the astral world. They have remained in the etheric vehicle, in a kind of limbo that ranges from milder forms of wandering in lonely darkness, to insensate craving, and efforts to obsess living persons who themselves are indulging in vices and activities similar to what they knew. In the annals of Spiritualism there are innumerable instances of this kind of testimony which renders the scene of life after death forbidding. But it must be remembered that this is not the universal condition, and that we see here again, fiction supplanting fact, because the concept of reincarnation has been rejected.

The Suicides

Nowhere is the difference between fact and fiction so startlingly illustrated as in the suicide cases. People who take their lives believe that they are getting out of their desperate situation, because death ends all. But any person who is tempted to take his life had better have a second look at what he may expect the next minute to hold for him. He is certain to find, to his astonishment, that he is not dead. Probably he will find himself standing there stupified, gazing upon his handiwork, unable to believe what he has done.* His condition will be one of overwhelming regret for an act that can never be reversed. If he has hung himself, the choking sensation will continue as long as he remains with the physical body—and he has a tendency to do just that. Since he cannot untie the rope around his neck, he has finally to realize that the physical body is dead, and he must abandon it. But this will not relieve him of the driving urgencies, the tensions, and anxieties that brought him to his terrible plight. The causes will still be there, experienced even more intensely than they were before death, while nothing can change the finality of the suicidal act. It is a serious position to be in, but even though it will be long-suffering, the forces that grip him will gradually wear away. It should be further noted about suicide, that the motive that prompted it, is the key factor determining the karmic results of the act. A noble motive, and a cruel selfish one, will result in different kinds of karma accordingly.

The Fiction of Capital Punishment

It can be readily understood, in the light of the knowledge presented in this book, that capital punishment does not remove the brutal criminal person finally from society. Although his physical incarnation has ended, after death he is attracted strongly by magnetic links to the same haunts and associates as before death. Moreover, driving him is the added virulence of hatred, derived from what he believes to have been injustices visited upon him.

*Reference Appendix p. 173.

His marauding nature can now become a persuasive influence from the etheric realm, through obsessing younger criminals, particularly those who can be drawn or compelled into more violent crimes. It would be better if such persons were not executed, but incarcerated, until they can be trained or otherwise aided to grow out of their present inclinations; because, in any case the training and disciplining will take place, here or hereafter.

Sudden Death

Violent deaths offer dramatic examples of unbroken waking consciousness that continues right through the experience of death and beyond. There are many vivid and instructive accounts available of experiences of sudden death, and what one immediately attempts to do thereafter. One needs only to look through reliable reports of psychical and spiritualistic records for such accounts. The following is an example:

Some years ago there was a Methodist minister in Chicago whose speciality was his overly vivid preaching about the condition those will inherit, who die in unrepentant sin. Repeatedly he urged that the only salvation for the soul was conversion as taught in his particular church. One evening he was disembarking from a commuter train with a crowd of other passengers who were hurrying home after the day's work. He rushed around the end of the train to cross the tracks, and stepped in front of an oncoming express train. He died instantly, and knew nothing of it except for a terrific pain in his chest which seemed to stay with him. He found himself immediately surrounded by a crowd of people who, to his great annoyance, were pushing him about. He hurried on his usual way homeward, and upon reaching the house, he entered, as always, only to find that his wife and children didn't seem to be aware of his presence, they apparently could neither see nor hear him. This astonishing state of affairs completely confused him. He could not understand what had happened. Finally, in a daze, he wandered away in darkness, continually being pushed by the crowd of people around him. It was years later, when, through the beneficent assistance of spiritual helpers, he was able to learn what really had happened to him. He found that he had died when the train struck him, and had been held earth-bound by the forces of his thinking and preaching of materialistic versions of punishment after death. The people around him, who were constantly pushing him, were actually the departed souls whom he had mis-informed as to what they could expect after death. They too, were in limbo, held there through their fanatical beliefs and fears, due to the teaching which they had faithfully followed. This preacher endured a long period of the conditions he himself had created and visualized for others. Later, after comprehending his situation, he awakened in his place in the astral world, and was able to occupy himself fully and happily thereafter in helping to guide others from that grim and dreary earth-bound stage, into the restful and blissful state that he found beyond it.*

Using Discrimination

In referring to material that has come via mediumistic sources from the other side of death, one must remember that no knowledge is to be embraced by anyone if it does not pass the test of one's own deeper reason and intelligence—this is not saying that the 'closed mind' should remain closed. One must judge the validity of any added knowledge by applying to it the understanding that has already been gained through knowledge of the universal principles and laws that prevail in the cosmic order. If new knowledge comes into conflict with one's understanding, it can be held tentatively until it grows under further

*"Thirty Years Among the Dead" - p. 307. Carl A. Wickland (This is among many such cases related.)

examination and application, or fades and is rejected. A good example of the need for discrimination is the contention held among some believers in reincarnation, that human beings can reincarnate as animals, or other strange mixing of forms, half animal, half human. That this is a fictitious supposition, is completely supported by the framework of universal principles and laws. The evolution of the Soul is an ongoing process. Once the human stage is attained, there can be no reversion of the Soul to a lower stage of evolution. What is possible is that of the greedy, lustful individual who craves only the pleasure of indulging in the vices of his physical life, and who finds himself after death in the helpless plight of the earthbound, may automatically shape the astral and etheric matter in his image, suggesting the kind of animality driving him. It is possible also for one whose bestiality drives him to do so, to obsess an animal temporarily. But it is a fiction that people reincarnate as swine, or cats, or rats; it is a fact that some of them act similarly, and may, in an earth-bound condition, actually resemble such appearances. Human souls do not reincarnate physically in the animal kingdom, although there may be astral resemblances of such cases.

Finally, it is no fiction that some occultists do develop the power to use the subtler bodies to project consciousness at a distance, passing through physical walls, walking through locked doors and other obstructions, without difficulty, in the service of Truth. They may go to the other side of the world, and even in other regions of time and space. Such powers are attained by the great Teachers who have mastered the esoteric structure of the Ancient Wisdom. They know well the inner worlds of Nature, and the wiser course to be pursued for a normal, happier way forward for humanity.

Let us now consider that very interesting next phase of the great cycle of reincarnation—the journey through the Astral World.

7

FAMILIAR JOURNEY IN THE AFTER-WORLDS

The Astral World

After death, you awaken in 'your place' in the astral world. You—the real you— have been there before, again and again. Its familiarity is recognizable through its strangeness. Imagine not having to eat, or keep warm, or cool, to seek shelter, or worry about buying clothes. There are no meteorological elements from which to be protected. Imagine all movement by you, so startlingly simple that you have only to visualize where you are going, and *will* yourself there—and there you are! You are clothed in what you imagine yourself to be wearing. Although people on earth may not openly mention that they entertain such ideas, I think that secretly we 'remember' that there is, or must be, such a place as the astral world. Going there, after a well-lived life, might be thought of as comparable to starting on a vacation some beautiful summer morning, driving along an open highway in a new car.

The world is lovely, and your worries have been left behind for the moment. If you are truly detached from the worrisome Earth scene, every moment brings fresh interest and happiness. This is somehow the way we feel an ideal vacation ought to be. Why? It may be because one instinctively associates an ideal vacation with 'release' from world pressures and uplifted with sheer happiness—the kind we have known in the astral world. One automatically associates a present ideal condition with an archetypal one remembered from somewhere in one's deep interior consciousness.

Will and Vision in the Astral World

The astral world seems strange to us, because the astral matter through which our consciousness acts is different from physical matter; it is less dense, more subtle, which means that it is infinitely more responsive to those powers of one's self that remain mostly latent, or are held in abeyance, in the physical world. Astral matter is more easily manipulated by the human will, and by powers of visualizing, than is physical matter. An architect who visualizes a house to be built on earth, has only begun to accomplish the objective. A contractor must be sought, and laborers hired to construct the house, in addition to obtaining the materials that have to be purchased and assembled. But in the astral world no such laborious procedure exists. One creates his own dwelling, if he must have one, by visualizing and *willing* it. Needless to say, an observer travelling there might find some imposing structures that are mostly facades, because the visualization had not been as complete and thorough as a physical plane house is. One who has been a housebuilder on earth will probably erect a grand house for himself in the astral world and, due to his habits on earth, he is likely to be found creating his materials before building the house.

But, with greater awareness of his powers, he might realize that in the astral world it is possible to create the whole house with the same energy used to create the materials.

It sounds ridiculous, nevertheless it is true, that an imagined automobile can be driven beautifully along an imagined road, even without an imagined engine! Do you not remember that there is—or must be—such an Alice-in-Wonderland-place in this universe, replete with para-doxes and illusions, a place where one begins to break free of the very idea of heavy physical limitation? It is our faint recollections of the astral plane, in my opinion, that cause us in the physical world to be so gullible—unless we are on our guard—to any display of powers of magic. We some-how know that one *should* be able to 'pull a rabbit out of a hat'.

Another major departure from our customary physical world thinking, is that in the astral world there is no such thing as ownership of astral property, or laws pertaining to possessions of any kind. In fact, the whole idea of to-getherness there, of both matter and form, is based on magnetism—magnetic attraction. Your own comes to you, and *is* yours. You receive by giving and serving. No one possesses anything by seizing and by forceful design. If you want to improve your domicile with a mountain view, you create it there.

Matter Responds to Our Powers

Movement in the astral world is by one's will, or by affinity with places, people, or conditions. One finds one-self immersed in atmospheres, because, consciously or unconsciously one has created them. We are drawn to our surroundings wherever we are, by what we are. Astrally, the creating is much more direct and immediate than it is in the physical world. A bibliophile quite naturally surrounds himself with beautiful books, a mechanic with ideal machines and tools. People arrive in the circles with which they have a natural affinity. Obviously the creative people—artists of every kind—find astral matter and life infinitely more malleable to their vision, than any condition that could possibly exist in the physical world. Beauty comes alive in subtlest ethereal forms, radiating sparkling joy wherever it manifests. There are no time-brackets within which things must be done. Happiness is not incarcerated within certain hours. One doesn't have to wrap up one's creativity and put it away until later, due to the arrival of tedious necessities to perform. It is a time-less world, or rather a world in which one creates one's own time. Old people grow younger in the astral scene. Children grow into blossoming youthfulness. Everyone becomes what he thinks he is, or would like to be—shoe-maker or king. A new arrival from the physical world who has spent years in a paralyzed condition in a wheelchair, can forget the chair, the crutches, and the medicine, and begin the new life without impediment. There is rest-fulness and freedom to do as one pleases. Is this heaven? Not yet.

A Darker Side

There is the darker side of the astral world. It is summed up in the idea of 'purging' or eliminating the attraction of the denser or coarser forms of attachments enjoyed while in the physical body. This process of dissociation from entanglements in the material world can be prolonged and painful. Many of the spiritualistic communications from the astral world reveal an extraordinarily dreary scene in a grey world after death*. Conditions can become appalling for the person who, for example, commits suicide through selfish motives, by attempting to escape justice, or be-

*Ref. Appendix pp. 171-172

cause he has lost control of his vehicles through becoming obsessed, and has fallen under some alien compulsion to take his life. The suicide cannot understand what happened; he expected to be dead, and finds himself very much alive. There are inebriates who died from their indulgences, and those who were on drugs and narcotics, whose cravings are magnified, with no possibility of satisfying them. In the astral world their suffering is excruciating until they are brought to understand their situation.*

There are many accounts in legitimate spiritualistic messages from the astral world, where those who pass through death's door first awaken in deep puzzlement, and sometimes terrible stress. Over and over these messages reiterate certain points that may evoke threads of memory in us, making the astral seem vaguely familiar as to what lies ahead, and the implications in it for the individual—this way that all of humanity must go.

Regarding messages through mediumship or psychics, a warning is sounded by H. P. Blavatsky and her Teachers, that is given further confirmation by leading students of Theosophy with respect to the delusive nature of the conditions that prevail in the astral world. If one is to discriminate among the myriad pieces of useful and useless information from all sources, and to evaluate them intelligently, there will have to be a basic knowledge of man's occult nature—his bodies and principles—and a sound general knowledge of the normal great cycle of reincarnation. Otherwise there will be a growing mass of confusing information offering borderland, and 'summerland', revelations as well as messages of painful experiences that people give after death, who are without purpose or repose. To this confusion is added the testimony from those who are advancing to greater heights in the spirit world, who deny vehemently that there is any such

*Ref. Appendix pp. 173-174

thing as reincarnation. The more vivid messages are from the earthbound dead who are wandering in limbo, empty of interest and activity, some of them with vague hopes of returning somehow, into a living body on earth.

What has been said regarding the astral world indicates that fear-stricken individuals are frightened by their own creations. If we insist upon horrifying ourselves for entertainment, manufacturing all kinds of demoniacal situations, peopled by dreadful beings and thought-forms, while we are here in the physical world, we are surrounding ourselves with these forms in the astral world, and will find them around us when we arrive there. A modern crime against childhood is the commercialized distortion of life's realities, through the propagation of violent terror tales that are being broadcast in these days. They evoke a faculty in the child's mind to imagine these, and even worse things, as reality. Somehow humanity must awaken fully to the truth that peace is created by being peaceful, and order by being orderly. If we are kindly, courageous and benign individuals ourselves, we will be surrounded by such company. But if we persist in generating thought-forms of malice, hatred, fear of one another, and distrust of life itself, we create that kind of life in the after-worlds, as well as on earth. This truism is only partly apparent in the physical world; but it is *absolute* in the astral world. The sooner we are able to recognize it, the happier will be the remainder of our journey of this incarnation, which—remember—includes not only the astral world experience, but the very much longer period of mental existence in what is termed the heaven-world, as will be noted in the next chapter.

It is very useful to have before one a comparison of certain basic knowledge of the sub-plane structure of both the physical and the astral worlds for added light upon the transition from the physical into the astral plane life. We will be able to perceive then, explanations for the strange differences between the astral and physical life, as we have been noting them. We must never lose sight of the fact that what is evolving everywhere in this universe are units of consciousness in human beings, animals, the vegetable and mineral kingdoms of life, and even in the ethereal and spiritual realms. Life is consciousness, and consciousness is life. Consciousness exists in units at all levels and stages of unfoldment, whether in atoms, human beings, stars, or universes. The totality of all is the One Supreme Consciousness that created and sustains the universe.

The Physical Sub-Planes

If we now think of the physical world as being the densest one—the 7th—of the seven planes of the universe, we observe in it, four recognizable subdivisions, namely: solid, liquid, gaseous, and a subtler medium— sometimes denoted *etheric*—through which sound-waves, light-waves, and electrical impulses pass. These four subdivisions are designated as four sub-planes of the physical plane. But, it is also an occultly known fact, that there are seven—not four—*sub-planes* in each of the seven great planes. Consequently, when we lump together everything beyond the gaseous level into one 'etheric' division, we are failing to give recognition to the other three subtler sub-planes of the physical plane. In this present accounting there are *four* etheric levels of invisible physical matter. They could be listed numerically, indicating that they are of increasing refinements of structure, or we might give them the designations listed by some theosophical writers as the *etheric, super-etheric, sub-atomic,* and *atomic* sub-planes. The latter is said to be region of the true ultimate atom of the physical plane. The difference between the physical and astral planes is due to the nature of the atoms of each plane. Those of the astral plane are as the electrons in a physical atom. They are different energy packets. The astral atom has a subtler quality and tone than has the physical, a rhythm that produces the distinct differences that are characteristic of the astral world.

Doorway of Transition

Man's etheric vehicle is composed of matter in the three higher physical sub-planes—the atomic, sub-atomic and super-etheric. They are intangible and invisible, but are still physical. These three sub-planes actually mark the locale of the transitional experience that takes place immediately before and after death, and prior to one's awakening in the astral world. In this etheric region of the physical world there is an exact replica of everything visible on the physical plane. Our etheric vehicles are exact duplicates of the physical body. When the physical body dies, consciousness is still encased in this etheric replica, or "double". This is the region where you will find 'earth-bound' people, that is to say, those who have departed from the physical world, but are consciously trying to cling to their material existence. They can see the world around them as we see it—the same houses, rooms, chairs, books, pictures on the wall, all are there just as known before death, except that they are replicas in another dimension. So far as consciousness is concerned, there is no absolute demarcation between the dense physical and etheric sub-planes. A certain amount of overlapping of influences exists where the sub-planes merge. Even though particles of all four physical sub-planes are present in the solid physical vehicle, there is a well marked division between the invisible etheric and the visible physical bodies; we see and contact the dense physical body, but are unaware of the etheric body. There is another qualification: the etheric body is not a separate vehicle of consciousness. It receives and distributes vital forces from higher planes, therefore is necessary to our physical health, and it plays the crucially important role of transmitting information and impulses between physical, astral and mental bodies, thus determining the kind of life we are having. We may be helped in realizing the condition, to visualize every solid, liquid and gaseous part of the physical body as surrounded and permeated with its etheric envelope of matter—its 'double', so to say. This produces the duplicate of the physical world at the etheric level.

The Actual Moment of Death

At death, the *Etheric Double* withdraws from the dense body, and is sometimes witnessed by sensitive people as a grey-violet mist that may condense into a figure which appears to be a replica of the expiring person. There is a glistening, delicate cord between the two forms, the physical and the etheric, referred to by occultists as the "silver cord". Its significance is that when this delicate cord snaps, actual death takes place, because the withdrawal of the etheric double has broken the last link that Man's higher consciousness has with the physical body. The integrating faculty that has heretofore unified all the parts, now leaves the body, and the physical vehicle becomes a mere bundle of independent cells. The cells no longer have allegiance to the central system of the body, but the life in them continues. The organs break down as the cell life runs rampant. The physical body seems to be even more alive after death—alive in particle units, but dead in its totality. As has been said: "The corpse would not decompose if all its parts were dead." All molecules which compose it are living, and tend to separate. When the etheric double finally quits the dense body, its tendency is to remain in the vicinity of the physical corpse until it, too, disintegrates, unless of course something such as a bomb explosion disintegrates the physical form. Withdrawal of the etheric double is usually accomplished in peaceful unconsciousness.

What to Avoid

But if, during this period of withdrawal, there is a strong emotional upset, such as fear or hate, or there is fierce attraction to the physical world, there will be delay in the full transition into the astral world. The departed one finds that he is held in the earth-sphere, yet will not be able to function in the astral world either. The grey condition surrounding him duplicates the physical world, but is not the same. It is a very unpleasant situation, in which people drift about lonely and frightened, in a gloomy fog, unable to communicate with anyone. They need help in understanding their plight and guidance toward freedom from it. This experience is often described in spiritualistic communications.* Normally, people are not conscious during the transition time. But if they are, they can through detachment, free themselves of the etheric matter. There are others, however, who are delayed within this limbo for long periods, even months and years. The best advice for them is to try to 'let go' the physical world, and with consciousness turned fully to the spiritual realms, and the mighty Beings who are there, move swiftly with full faith into the Light.

When the human consciousness passes on fully into the astral world, the etheric double, in its turn, becomes a disintegrating vehicle. Etheric wraiths are sometimes seen in graveyards, and such places. In all cases where people cling desperately to physical existence, the astral body cannot become completely separated from its ethe-

*"The Search for Bridey Murphy", pg. 142 by Morey Bernstein, 1956 Hutchinson and Co. Ltd., Great Britain

ric shell, therefore it remains aware only of its etheric surroundings.

Fortunately, the fact is that this process of transition into full astral consciousness does take place in time—for everyone. In our materialistic age many people are glamorized by worldly attractions, and in addition to their lack of knowledge as to what to expect, are confused in the early stages after death. It is here that loving friends and relatives on the other side, as well as among the living, have an opportunity to help those who are in difficulty.

Seven Astral Sub-Divisions

The astral plane has its seven sub-divisions corresponding to the physical plane's seven. Thus the lowest astral sub-plane, is of the densest matter, and one will find there the coarsest conditions and creatures. Its juxtaposition to the physical earth, places it slightly below the physical ground level. The unfortunate beings in that region experience darkness and perpetual night, filled with evil horrors—a truly 'Dantean hell'. The most materialistic have sunk into this state in the toils of their cravings, hatreds and violent cruelties. All spiritual impulses have been lost, and even the link with the immortal consciousness has been dissolved. Around them are sluggish primeval conditions of dullest life-consciousness. In this lowest astral region will be found the once-human creatures who have turned against the tide of evolution, and through age-long practices of evil, have lost the last traces of human-ness, and spirituality. They are life's nethermost failures, that are slowly disintegrating in Nature's cauldron that re-cycles useless material into primordial pristine matter. Meanwhile, the immortal element in such creatures has returned to its monad to prepare a new venture into evolution, for the monad is imperishable. But the usual 'hells' are made and transcended by individuals who, trapped by their iniquities, can be liberated by the spark of divinity innate in themselves.

Less dense is the sixth sub-plane; it coincides with the physical surface. Found there, are all who are strongly bound in patterns of their past worldly preoccupations and ways of thinking, their routine concerns with earthly affairs. For a considerable time they may hover about their former business places, and situations with which they had been associated on earth. They remain conscious of many things in connection with these. A point to remember, however, is that they are not contacting actual physical matter itself, but the astral counterpart of it. They are surrounded by astral counterparts of everything physically existing, including geographical features. During the early part of astral life, the people there are not yet free of the sensate habits and customs that they cultivated in their past incarnation. Often, these people will be found suffering intensely from frustrations. In addition to human creatures in the lower astral sub-planes, there are elemental and non-human forms of life, some aspects of it, as on earth, being anti-human. The astral world also swarms with thought-forms both good and evil. However, the evil influences are no part of our consciousness unless we attract them. Here, indeed, a person is truly as he thinks and feels he is. The pure in heart are shielded by their own atmosphere.

As consciousness rises higher in the next two sub-planes, the fifth and the fourth, all contact with the physical plane fades away. In these and the higher —the third and second sub-planes —the landscapes of the astral world are largely created by the humanity located there. This feature provides the possibility for creating all sorts of conditions that the superstitious beliefs and faiths of people have led them to imagine—the 'Valhallas', the 'Happy Hunting-Grounds', the 'Elysian Fields', and so on. Inhabitants reaching there are dwelling in their places, they are enjoying life in astral homes, schools, cities, creating surroundings according to their imagination as they work through the longer or shorter period of attachment to materiality. They are concerned with realities of the astral world, adding their contribution to the structures they have inherited. Normally, everyone after death passes through the sub-divisions of the astral plane, consciously or unconsciously. The grosser particles of astral matter are constantly being left behind and falling away, as one rises into higher spheres. Those who are advancing higher, are gradually eliminating all attachment to their past materialistic conditions on earth. They are becoming etherealized, thus refining and purifying their denser nature. When at last they reach the seventh, the highest sub-plane in the astral world, they are preparing to enter the heaven-life. They are thoroughly spiritual-minded and may spend long periods in intellectual, artistic, and other creative pursuits and expressions of their higher nature. Some great geniuses, in fact, may work out in detail, in the more malleable astral matter, particular devices that may later become inventions by someone—or even by themselves, upon their return to earth. Great ideas and works of art have had their origin in this manner.

The effect of the law of reincarnation upon the normal tidal flow inward, becomes ever more marked, the higher the level reached in the after-worlds. Earth attraction is strongest at the densest level. Many years and centuries may pass before the reincarnating soul returns to earth. All progress is inward to more spiritual levels. The transcension is irresistible. This is why spiritualists usually contend that there is no reincarnation; that there is only evolvement upward.

During the whole period that the person is in the astral world, he is within the region of possible recall by earth influences. It is possible for some strong stimulus of grief or selfish desire by a loved one on earth, to reach and draw him into limited communication through some medium or agency. But this can be done only with stress to him. That this is a disservice to the departed can be understood, when it is realized that they are in the process of freeing themselves from physical and lower astral attraction, in preparation for entering the heaven-world. Any pull back to earth is a retarding disturbance.

Looking back, we might say, in summary, that each person awakens in the condition in the astral world, that he has created for himself by the life he has just finished living. If he has permitted himself to indulge only in satisfying appetites, and his craving for material possessions, and obtaining the wherewithal for these, meanwhile cultivating coarse and vulgar tastes and habits, he can expect to find himself awake in the astral world in those conditions that will frustrate and reverse this way of life. The change required is to become disenthralled with all those desires and enmeshments. He will wear out these baser desires through frustration in order that greater realities may be experienced in finer, purer, happier conditions.

Learn Before Departure

People who have not taken the trouble to learn about the astral plane and its phenomena before they reach there, are likely to be unnecessarily disturbed by the altered conditions they experience upon their arrival. Death sweeps all of us willy-nilly into this strange land, this new geography of the Self. It is only sensible to acquaint ourselves with its main features and modes of existence, and to know what to expect before departing on our journey into it. It will be a blessing to find upon arrival there, conditions that we have some familiarity with, for we will know what to do with ourselves, instead of being a helpless burden upon others. In fact, we can be among those who can give loving assistance to the fear-driven arrivals, who are devoid of inner resources and are in need of aid.

If the general idea can be grasped of the absolute need for disenthrallment from materiality after death, it will be seen that the greater spiritual teachers of the world have tried to cultivate in man the habits and ways of life that will lead him into a happier, swifter, less painful and more constructive transition into the after-world conditions, where he will spend the greater part of each incarnation. They taught the happier way of life in view of the whole span of an incarnation, including its longer cycles. And those who have depicted for us in all its more lurid aspects the hells we've heard of, no doubt drew inventive inspiration from what can be seen in the lowest sub-division of the astral regions.

There is beautiful assurance that average, good people drop into peaceful sleep at death, passing through both the etheric transition, and lower astral conditions in blissful unconsciousness. They are like people in a jet plane flying high over a city and are totally unconscious of any slum areas and loathsome degradations that they might be passing over far below. Perhaps, based upon facts, there is a wisdom in the ancient prayer: "Lord, deliver us from sudden death", because very often consciousness remains awake for a time when ejected suddenly from the body. But even under this condition, the informed will know what to do.

Unless there is need for a mission of service in the lower astral worlds, they are to be shunned, for the same reasons that the lowest, most degraded physical environments are to be avoided, unless necessary. Above and beyond them is the joyous life, with its endless opportunities to serve and learn while one is preparing for entrance once more into the heaven-world.

8

HEAVEN AGAIN

The Profound Withdrawal

From the astral world one passes into the 'shining land'—the heaven world—sometimes called *Devachan*, and there one reaches the culminating period of an incarnation. The permanent harvesting now takes place of the essence of all that was experienced in the life on earth. Having completed both the physical involvement in materiality, and the astral disenthrallment from its attachments, consciousness is then able to give utmost concentrated attention to the mental world, and to dwell impersonally in the permanent meaning of each experience, as well as its ramifications. This is a most valuable time of recapitulation and the rendering of experience into faculty.

Every mental interest that a person has had on earth, particularly his deeper interests in Truth, in high ideals and aspirations, all open fresh doorways to mental vistas beyond what was perceived on earth. Here, at last, is the place for unobstructed concentration in a peace that ensures comprehension of the full meaning of what did happen to one on earth. It is as though while living on earth one half-glimpses things and opens any number of puzzling doorways, gathers many seed ideas, all of which are sown in the mind to remain there inactive until developed in devachan. And when one arrives there, with all the time needed to devote uninterrupted attention to every point of contact one has had, these can be explored and developed to the fullest, and the most profound meaning perceived in each experience.

A Second Death

One first awakens in devachan, possessed of a vitality, a vivid clarity of perception, and an unimpeded radiance of life and being that can only be imagined on earth. While a person is in the physical body using the physical brain the flow of inner life is limited in repressive ways, the body ever demanding attention to its incessant needs and frequent calamities—the brain, its fixations. Free of both, in devachan, the person achieves a kind of apotheosis of what he believes he *can* be, or at least dreams he *should* be. Life is far more vivid in the mental plane, than anything experienced in the physical, because it is two planes nearer to Reality.

Departure from the astral world has sometimes been referred to as a 'second death', but the transition takes place gently, with no disturbance, anxiety or sorrow of any kind. The actual change is again experienced as though one were falling into a glorious sleep. The astral life dims out, as one becomes unconscious while certain adjustments are made in the shuffling off the 'mortal coils' of the astral body. The mental world is totally different from the astral world. Its atoms are of a different measure, and respond to faculties of consciousness of their order. The adjustments that take place are concerned with the centering of consciousness in a vehicle that is fundamentally different from anything in the lower levels. For one thing, the phenomenal re-arrangement of astral atoms in their concentric shells of matter from densest to finest which occurred in the astral body, confining the discarnate person to 'his place' in the astral world, does not happen at all in the mental world. This fact is of considerable significance.

Paving the Road to Heaven

Mentally one is, as he *is*. Each person is at the stage to which he has evolved his mental faculties. If he is a mechanic, a writer, or a priest, his mental outlook and spiritual content have already paved his way into heaven. Each one of us creates, while on earth, his spheres in heaven. He passes into the particular mental level that corresponds precisely to his stage of evolution, and remains oriented there throughout his heaven life. Although he explores as fully as possible, every avenue that he opened in his incarnation, he does not progress to higher levels than that which he has provided. No one leaps beyond himself mentally, either here or in heaven; he grows in his power to perceive and comprehend within the limits of his evolved faculties. The quality of mental substance that forms the mind is as it has been evolved. The richer one's mental and spiritual life on earth has been, the more extensive will be his heritage in heaven. Endless are the infinitudes of the mental plane which indeed border upon and open into the cosmic realms that reflect the Divine Mind. The possibilities offered on earth, in the pursuit of Truth that can fructify in the heaven-life, has little or no recognition as yet.

Worldly people who have been wholly absorbed in the practical side of things while on earth, who have interested themselves, for example, altogether in the machinery and the mechanical appliances of life, naturally will not provide as many intellectual and perceptive doorways for Self-realization as they might, had they been otherwise occupied. The opportunity for a rich heaven-life exists while we are on earth, using the incarnation to explore pathways to Truth, while gaining wide experience through many relationships. A magnificent heaven-life is not suddenly brought about after arrival in devachan. Those who reach there with narrow outlooks and limited spiritual resources, whose lives on earth were devoid of any interest in—or expression of—the life of the spirit, are able to make only slight use of the wondrous advantages of devachan. Theirs will be a sleep in nirvanic bliss. But one who has cultivated many avenues of the spirit—the service of humanity, art, philosophy, music, metaphysics and religion, or who has felt strongly attracted to the masters and teachers in any of the great fields of activity, will find in the resources of the heaven world the supreme experience of this incarnation. The beneficent communion with Reality blossoms, with full comprehension of all knowledge gained in the past, thus unveiling ways to future attainment.

Beyond the Shadow of Evil

No evil, nor threat of evil, can touch the dweller in devachan. Even the memory of evil disappears, which blessed culmination alone assures complete rest during the heaven-life. The important difference between life in the heaven world, and anywhere else in man's experience, is simply that the vehicles of the mortal personality that incur desires, dissentions, disharmony and death, have all been purified, dissolved and left behind during the purgation in the astral world. Only the finer mental material now envelopes the immortal Self. And this vehicle is employed only with selfless thoughts, deeper wisdom, and nobler aspirations to Truth. The devachanee has reached a condition that responds only to the highest influences possible for him. This characteristic exclusion of all passional elements that marks one's entry into devachan makes impossible, by its nature, any evil or sorrow reaching his present situation. There is a complete orientation of life to the immortal Soul. Therefore, every aspect of incarnational experience, both good and what appeared to be adverse, are now seen as different aspects of what was necessary in unfolding the Divine Life within. Only the constructive good is revealed in every experience. One's friends and closest people are all present in the heaven-life in their ideal form. Their presences are glorified by their own immortal selves, rendering the beloved ones even more wondrous, more beautiful, than ever known on earth, communion with them is perfect at this level. Although this seems to be illusory, it is actually greater reality, for only the ideal of every relationship is present, and the ideal is closest to Reality.

The Permanent Attainment

This final lengthy stage of an incarnation ends in the greater glory that radiates from the inmost realms of the Soul. Perhaps we on earth may attribute to some lingering memory of this reality in devachan, the awareness that is shown in all healthy people of good will, that somehow all *is* well, despite threats of dire calamity in the surrounding gloom. It would be only natural that, with many incarnations ending in reunion with the Soul, the deep impressions would remain within us throughout each incarnation, quietly yet persistently shedding a heart-warming influence from within. Since the time spent in the heaven world is by far the longest period of one's life-span, it is only reasonable to suppose that impressions gained in devachan must be the basis of one's awareness of truth's direction at any time. Knowing how difficult it is to describe Nature's beauty and harmony as perceived in the physical world, no one can expect to do more than refer to the realities that are known in the heaven world. The beauty and ecstasy that appear spontaneously at times in one's life and work on earth, may well be echoing faintly the life known in devachan.

The permanent attainment in heaven, is the transmutation of one's earth life experiences into moral, mental and spiritual faculties for the next life on earth. These developments are not in terms of memory, but of unfolded capacities. In devachan, the mental material itself is entirely used up, and the vehicle itself disintegrated. This is a reminder that all three bodies, physical, astral, and mental, belong to the past incarnation. The essential qualities in that personality's transiencies are totally digested and rendered into ability and faculty. The immortal Soul remains, and has grown with the harvesting of all that has taken place. Experiences come and go; capacities are retained. The process is one of extracting the nectar of growth-consciousness out of the fruitful experiences of mortal life. Every last drop of experience is precious material conveyed to the immortal Self.

Devachan is a universal inheritance. In the cycles of reincarnation, it is as necessary to the Soul as sleep is to the mortal man. There are certain exceptions. First, there are the spiritually advanced people who, throughout a series of rapid reincarnations are engaged in special work in some connection with the cycles of evolution on this planet. Other extraordinary exceptions are those people who are making karmic adjustments with the timing of other persons coming into incarnation and with whom they will experience relationships. This is possible with an early death and quick reincarnation. Also included among exceptions there are those cases of the earth-bound, the unevolved, and those who remain in the earth-sphere or lower astral planes until reincarnated. We must also recognize that there are some who are utterly depraved, and some who are evil and who have cut themselves off from anything other than the lowest astral level. Where they seek coarser and more brutal experiences. Also from this region come examples of the worst elements of satanism, obsession of those of evil inclination, or even of some unwary psychic sensitives.

There are, of course, other exceptions which would be individualized reasons and not numerous enough to warrant going into each and every possibility at this point. There are, as I suggested above, a number of reasons for rapid reincarnation some that include more advanced, and even highly developed, people as well.

Time-Spans in the Timeless

We arrive now at the uncertain question of the length of time spent in devachan. It may be of help in giving some idea regarding relative times, to point to a guiding principle: the conservation of energy as applied to mortal man's tri-plane existence. No energy is ever lost; it is either transposed, or stored. Whatever is generated must produce its effect somewhere. It may remain stored until the opportunity arrives for releasing it. Generated energies can, and are, transposed between planes. In the intra-plane energy transpositions the law of cause and effect is still operative. For example, all of the generated forces (energies) which are mental in nature will have their effect and release in the mental world. Consequently, the total time spent in devachan is related to the wealth of mental experiences brought from the earth life. In heaven there is perfect release. The length of time spent there depends upon the measure and quality of mental causes that were set in motion. People with the highest ideals and aspirations while on earth, who are not able to realize all of them in the physical world, have generated forces that are stored energies in the astral and mental levels. If no opportunity arrives before, for their release while on earth, they will be released finally in devachan. The interplay and use of these forces is not something that necessarily happens far away and distant in time. We are inhabiting the mental world in our mental body at present. And in this sense, heaven is all about us *now*. We could enter it at any time, in the degree to which we develop a pure nature and the faculty of withdrawing the Soul from sense-limitations.

Estimates of the actual time spent there are confronted with the difficulty of measuring time in a timeless world, or, in the timeless state of consciousness in that world. However, some comparative figures are available that have been set up through clairvoyant observations. Among these are the heaven-life spans of advanced Souls who are deliberately treading a way in life that leads to liberation from all necessity for reincarnation. It was observed that such Souls normally spend 1,000 to 2,000 years in Devachan.* A special research that was made into past lives of some 250 individuals revealed that they could be classified into 2 groups with spans of 700 and 1,200 years between lifetimes. These relative time-spans were followed consistently through vast periods of the past.** If we use the higher figures as a basis for comparison, one might reasonably expect that the more cultured normal people of self-disciplined and professional pursuits, such as scientists, artists, teachers, rulers and priests, would spend perhaps around 1,000 years in devachan.

Compared with these, the vast number of educated, well-meaning and dutiful people, would be likely to spend 600 to 1,000 years in devachan, with the probability that anywhere up to 25 years of this time would be spent in the astral world, and the remainder in devachan. As we glance down the scale of people who are preoccupied with the more earthly material aspects of life, the time spent in devachan is proportionately briefer. At the bottom of the

*"The Mahatma Letters to A. P. Sinnett", (Third & Revised Ed.) p. 173.
**Works of C. W. Leadbeater. 1910-11-12.

scale would be the most primitive human beings on earth, with little time or opportunity for other than maintenance of physical existence and whose life expectancy on earth is something like 30 - 40 years. The time spent in devachan would thereby be shortened. Practically *all* of the time would be used in the astral world. Such people necessarily reincarnate quickly, somewhere between 50 - 100 years after their death. Even though selfish, animal passions do not enter devachan, every human being, however primitive, does have faint stirrings of love and tenderness, of spiritual hopes and longings. These are as seeds that will find their growth in the higher astral world, as well as in devachan. There are to be expected, numerous exceptions to these general observations. But, one can understand that practically all human beings inevitably go to their 'heaven', even if briefly. Judging from this line of reasoning, those individuals in our present-day world whose minds are almost wholly fixed upon material joys and mechanical aids to happiness, are probably shortening their devachanic life, and lengthening the astral time it will take to disentangle consciousness from these more intense attractions to mundane appurtenances.

Communion - Not Communication

People in the heaven world are not in direct touch with friends or affairs on earth. They could not know of present calamities that might be taking place in this world. It is only via the immortal Self that they have any communion. This means that all situations and conditions are viewed and judged through the eyes of the Soul—beyond fear and sorrow, and wholly immersed in spiritual values.

The effects of a spiritual life that was lived on earth attracts, in devachan, attention from higher Intelligences. Forces radiating from them will stimulate spiritual faculties for future world use. Therefore, anyone performing extraordinary spiritual service on earth, can, through higher relationships in devachan, actually make fresh progress in his heaven-life. An inventive person can dream of new machinery and inventions that will later be developed on earth. After all, such dreams and thoughts become mental forms that may be picked up and used by an inventor on earth, someone who is in rapport with the dreamer in heaven.

In the light of this knowledge about the other side of death, it can be understood that one who has reached devachan cannot be recalled to earth by spiritualistic methods; neither will he be found wandering in some grey etheric level seeking futilely to understand where he is, or searching frantically for some means to reincarnate.

Universal Order

Order reigns supreme in the Universe, and therefore, in the depths of the immortal Soul. He who remembers, however faintly, the inner things, will not be diverted from his knowledge while on earth by any horror or woe, or by the glazed stare of death. He knows full well that life sings with two voices: Nature's transient tones that always come to harmonious rest, and 'Heaven's Song of Reality', heard in rhythms sublime and everlasting.

Normal reincarnation is life's swift method for the evolution of consciousness. To perceive this clearly, we have only to imagine the predicament of one who lived out the entire span of his incarnation on earth, lasting say 1,000 years, in the physical body alone! His consciousness would become stultified again and again in habitual patterns of sluggish inertia. These would alternate with whirlpools and storms of furious enthrallments, that would sink again in age-long ennui and weariness. His chances of spiritual progress would be blocked on every side by memories, and the burdensome awareness of limitations endured in physical life. Added to this, there would be unlimited opportunities to slip into evil tendencies and indulgences that, through karmic effects, could bar his progress for further ages to come.

Compare this with the truly wondrous mechanism of life, death, and reincarnation, that at the conclusion of a few decades of embodiment in physical form, life alternates, with the period of centuries required to slough away limitations, and evil tendencies. Thus, the very memory is closed off, and the Self is recharged with good influences, leaving only the whisper of conscience to guide one through a new life, freshly reborn. Contemplating this, one can only realize that if there be a God whose beneficent and ever-gentle hand is guiding his nurslings, it is here displayed ceaselessly with the manifold demonstrations that occur in the great rhythms of reincarnation.

9

THE INDESTRUCTIBLE SELF

As the heaven period reaches its conclusion, and its wondrous atmosphere, peopled with the most loved presences in one's universe, thins and dissolves, there dawns a yet more glorious reality. *You*, the Immortal, are there, so to speak, greeting you the mortal traveller who went forth into the worlds of separativeness, and have now returned to union in splendor. The profound metamorphosis takes place: complete union with the higher Self. The purified Self-consciousness remaining after the last traces of mortality disappears in devachan then merges self with immortal Self in the triumphant realization that this inmost splendor shining am "I", truly and forever. The inner core of the individual has been purged temporarily of all illusory attachment to life in the material worlds, and having reached peace without stain, he enters the indestructible Wholeness that knows no part-ness. This union with the higher Self is the culmination of a single great cycle of reincarnation.

The Soul briefly glimpses, in a state of timelessness, the long cycling way of death that has been trod from the measureless unreality to this Wholeness of Being. But the reincarnating Self is not yet liberated from life in the worlds of form, even though temporarily resting in freedom. Final liberation will come only when he has attained complete freedom from all bonds of attachment to material existence.

Thus are the truths to be exhumed from the Archaic Wisdom, that primordial body of enlightenment that is ever present in the world, and rediscovered from age to age. It exists almost as though it were some cosmic memory fossilized in the very rock foundations of the earth. From this most Ancient Wisdom of the world, the precious ore is supplied, revealing that Man descends from above, in order that he may evolve from below his latent divinity of power and love and creative fire, revivifying and releasing what was buried within his nature from the beginning—the spark struck from the Flaming Whole.

The Seventh Heaven

The scene in which the events of union occur, the cosmic geography, is that of the highest of the seven sub-planes of the mental plane. Devachan is a definite region in those seven sub-planes. The four denser ones are characterized by the form-building qualifications of mental matter, as stated previously in Chapter Four. Life there continues to be subordinated to form, and it is in this region of matter that we find the actual locale of devachan. The three higher levels, as explained, are of an entirely different character, being composed of matter that does not respond to form-building influences. This means that matter is subordinated to life in the higher levels of the mental plane. Life alters form at every moment. Forms are changed with every change of thought. Life is predominant. In the denser mental levels where life creates forms, there is more difficulty in manifesting subtler qualities through the forms, because of the rigidity of matter. At the physical level, far below, we know that matter becomes grossly rigid so far as man's will is concerned.

You can't *will* yourself to walk physically through a wall of your room; you will have to use the door. However, on the astral plane you can will the self to go through walls. As we rise above the physical, to the astral and mental matter, their substances have an increasing malleability and radiance not known in the denser matter. As the immortal Soul becomes increasingly liberated from the imprisoning density of matter—even that of devachan— there is glorious awareness of a freedom that is impossible in the worlds below. One is no longer limited to those windows that were necessary in the lower worlds in order to look out upon spiritual realities; one is immersed now in Reality itself. One dwells temporarily in formless cosmic horizons, aware of one's path in evolution, the purpose of life, and one's duty with respect to it. The after-death stages, as experienced, have been successive liberations from imprisonment in matter, each one demonstrating clearly that one never grows less through dying.

Access to Unlearned Knowledge

We have been reviewing the passage of the Self through its experiences in material bodies—physical, astral and mental—and in so doing have kept before us the fact that all three of the lower vehicles are mortal. Each was destined from birth to die. They are expendable, disposable garments, nothing more. But during the lifetime that the reincarnating Self spent in each of these bodies, the experiences opened windows of consciousness through which Reality could be glimpsed, particularly in devachan, where one's assessment of Truth could be adjusted. This feature can also awaken flashes of cosmic memory in the Self. These illuminations may play an important part in a future physical incarnation. For it is by inner intuitions, which spring from cosmic memory, that a person recovers unlearned knowledge through his immortal Soul, and from beyond—that is, from his realized union with God.

The Immortal Soul

The Immortal Soul, as we have seen, is seated in an actual vehicle, the causal body. This so-called 'body' is not a form, but it does have location, content, and continuity. Therefore the Soul is established in its center which does not perish in the cycles of time. It is a center of radiance composed of ultimate atoms of the mental plane. Not only does the causal body retain the enduring elements of Man's life, but nurtures their future use as well. From this treasury of past experience, immortal memories are awakened that become increasingly influential as the Soul evolves. In primitive man, the Soul registers but faintly. Later in evolution, as the Soul grows, it awakens latent powers that become more fully active in sensitive, creative individuals.

As we have seen, the Soul's consciousness is triune in its nature. Its three principles, manas, buddhi and atma, have received attention by various writers. Further information regarding these principles can be obtained from a number of source books.* *Manas* is that higher division of the mind that deals with Truth and creative vision. *Buddhi* is the love-irradiated wisdom that springs intuitively from beyond the mind and unites individual consciousness with life in all other forms through the bonds of love. *Atma* is the Soul's highest aspect, reflecting the will toward perfection. Its outstanding quality is that absolute lawfulness of being that is necessary to transmit safely the power of the Logos. Its virtue is indestructibility.

The magnificence of the Triune Soul fully awakened has

*See Reincarnalia, p. 185 for list of books on this subject.

121

no comparison on earth; its beauty has no equal here; its wisdom is the profoundest mystery of its being; its powers are awesome in prospect. 'Nearer than breathing' is the Soul, while simultaneously it races across star horizons in timeless, spaceless, omnipresence, yet is it ever centered imperishably in the One Creator of All.

Seeing the Future

From the immortal Soul's lofty viewpoint, the evolutionary plan is known. Its next karmic adjustments are beheld. The environmental and hereditary limitations are glimpsed; the objectives to be attained are clear. Flashes of Soul-memory have a large part to play in all this. Soul-memory is responsible for those deepest immutable convictions about right and wrong that seem to be innate in an individual, particularly in his abstract ideas of truth, justice, love and beauty. The individual Soul beholds, while in that paradise that exists beyond devachan, its eternal anchorage in the cosmic order, despite all fear and darkness that may be encountered in any coming mortal incarnation.

The Trinities

The Soul trinity directly reflects the Logoic Trinity. There is no stage above or below where the chain of trinities is broken. There is no trinity that does not reflect and merge into trinities above and below. All trinities of consciousness are links in the spiritual chain of union that is the Eternal Self. The trinity of the Soul merges at its lower level, manas, with the mental body of man's mortal trinity. And at the Soul's higher level, the Atma of its trinity, merges with the Para-atma of the higher Trinity. The *consciousness* of Para-atma is *Paramatman*—the Supreme Logoic Consciousness in its third aspect. The Para-atma is the monad turned outward, (turned inward, it

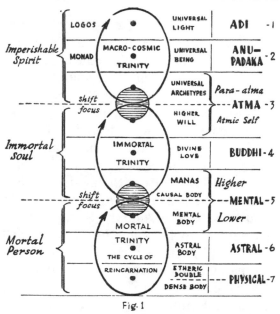

Fig. 1

LADDER OF TRINITIES TO GOD-CONSCIOUSNESS

"dwells in the bosom of God"). It is one of the myriad sparks, or monads, projected by the Logos into the Archetypal Creation. This is the absolute source of individual consciousness as projected by the Logos. The Para-atma is the *Authentic Existant* of Plotinus*, the blueprint for individualized perfection, the objective for an individual monad's vast evolutionary journey. Some have said that the universe was created for the evolution of the monads, which exist as a unity. Each is a particularized spark of consciousness within the all-pervading consciousness of the Triune Logos. Together, these monads at the conclusion of evolution, become again the One in the perfect harvesting of the universe. Meanwhile they endure fragmented separativeness in their outward-turned evolutionary unfoldment.

*Plotinus, The Third Ennead, 7th Tractate: *Time and Eternity.*

The Indestructible Self

All of this is to say that there exists a perfect type of each one of us. It is born directly of the will of God, and exists truly as a 'Father in heaven', in the precise meaning of that term. From that archetypal source springs the eternal drive onward to achieve excellence. This urge, in some respects is experienced by every living thing in the evolutionary scheme. The Soul itself was born of this drive. Slowly the Atma-buddhi-manas unit had to be evolved, and sustained as a unit by the power of the Divine Spirit, ever-flowing from the model that is gleaming as some aurora borealis in the archetypal world. The Spirit gives birth to the Soul, and the Soul grows through cycles of mortal life to become the glorified Self that unites Soul and Spirit. Influences from the archetype reach mortal man's consciousness as intuitive guidance along his path in life. If we are to be true to ourselves in the stresses around us, we must obey that light from within at all costs.

In its 'Seventh Heaven', the Soul is in the atomic level of the mental plane, where its highest principle—the Atma—is in a direct alignment of the causal body, Atma and Para-Atma. The memory of this alignment becomes awareness in the Soul of the reign of universal law in the schemes of evolution. This awareness may include the mighty Adepts who represent the governing forces of law in the unfolding evolution on earth. Clearly, it is from the atmic principle of the Soul that genius is awakened in the great individual; it is from there that the hero is inspired, the saint exalted, and the Illuminati enlightened with their revelations.

The Great Cycle Terminates

We have noted the terminus of an incarnation, the close

of a single great cycle of reincarnation.* Death and rebirth have followed each other through the many smaller cycles. And each time the Soul has gazed upon the scene of endless change from heights of changelessness. Each time it has experienced what binds and what emancipates the Self. Complete rest and renewal have come with the dissolution of the mortal person. With each new cycle the immortal Self comes forth strengthened, clearer in its purpose, comprehending more fully its three-fold being, knowing what to be aware of and what to seek. With the close of the great cycle, the Soul is prepared for a new role.

It is in that exalted region of union with the indestructible Self that a new incarnation truly begins. Pressures developing from the archetype turn the attention of the Self again to mortality; there is thirst for limitation. The urgency of desire comes from below, and the spiritual drive, from above. The necessity to continue growing through confinement within limitations, is joined with the dominant drive and direction that together shape the destiny ahead. Another incarnation will now begin to take place.

*This ideal presentation does not apply fully to everyone, everytime.

10

DAWN OF A NEW INCARNATION

Why Do We Reincarnate?

Was ever a clearer reason given than that of the poet's "Oh, my Beloved, fill the Cup that clears today of past regrets and future fears . . ."?* Quite simply, we reincarnate because we desire ardently this scene of non-recollectedness in a walled-in garden of blossoms with its illusion of privacy.

Step by step we have traced man's after-death withdrawal of consciousness, retiring upwards to its apotheosis of spiritual realization. And now, we are to consider the return into limitation. The proposition immediately presents a complex pattern of arrangements that nevertheless can be viewed simply because of the obvious unity of the whole structure. At any point we can *expect* to find what is next because of the integrity of the pattern. Moreover, the criterion of ordered Beauty is ever-present. Where Beauty is absent Truth is distorted and misrepresented; Truth anywhere is clothed in Beauty. As the song of a lark, so is the descent of the Soul into the worlds of form.

*Omar Khayyám - *The Rubáiyát, st. 21.*

The pattern of downward-turning, parallels the awakening of a healthy body with the dawning of a new day, in that it commences with a hunger for nourishment—a thirst for the wine of mortal sovereignty. The soul that is ready for reincarnation after the halcyon days in devachan, experiences a strong magnetic attraction for new life in physical form. This inner urgency has had recognition in the past, as the term *Tanha* indicates. 'Tanha' is an ancient Pali word meaning thirst for renewed experience. If one asks, 'why do we reincarnate?' or 'why do we return to Earth?', perhaps tanha suggests the true answer. There is the additional answer: 'unfinished business!' With a glance at how far we are from evolving in ourselves the Perfect Man, obviously there remains much living to be experienced by everyone.

Tanha

What exactly is this thirst for life? A superficial attention to the word 'tanha' will yield only a limited understanding of its implications. One can make the extremely interesting proposal, for example, that the 'thirst' also proceeds from the future. This allusion has a ring of Truth, because it directs attention to the actuality of an archetypal Self. Obscurity necessarily surrounds such a remote field of enquiry. Yet the magnetic pull from this source is primary at the point of the Soul's departure into a new incarnation. And its position of importance justifies adoption in our frame of understanding, of the existence of an archetypal universe, as was suggested in Chapter 4. We can reduce this vast subject with its complex ramifications to the simplistic proposition that life's evolution, its maintenance of organic and spiritual continuity that is in harmony with its ceaseless expansion, requires a pattern of perfection. The projection of an archetypal universe in life's subtlest regions is essential to the attainment in matter of an evolved reflection of the perfect universe.

Passive as this metaphysical conjecture may seem, the reality of the archetypal Self in Man springs to life positively, as magnetic force, in the Soul's consciousness, when devachan closes. The archetypal influence is the initial compelling factor urging reincarnation; it is actually the 'developmental norm', or 'goal' that manifests as a resistless pull of the future in the ongoing evolution of the Soul.

The grandeur of the great Archetypal Plan as a cosmic goal, lies in its scheme of perfection for everything that is evolving in the universe. This 'scheme' for every man is a divine destiny, the obedience of which is mandatory for the evolving Soul. The obedience is a spiritual duty that spreads from root to trunk to limb. We sometimes refer to "one's duty to oneself"—meaning usually, to one's general welfare. But the obedience intended here is far more profound, being that of mortal man to his immortal Soul which in turn is obedient to its archetypal Self. No single word seems to convey the full meaning required for such an understanding. Rather than seeking clumsily to invent one, we have used, in chapter 5, the Indian idea of dharma, the Sanskrit term that expresses precisely the sense of duty in any one to his higher Self, or his spiritual goal.

The two basic factors that govern the course of a reincarnation, are the forces of dharma and karma. The initial pull of dharma is woven indistinguishably into the fibres of karma. This latter prescribes the immediate limitations within which the reincarnated person is impelled to labor. The limitations are the computerized summation of his actions in the past, determining both the good and bad fortune that will attend the rebirth.

At this point, there is a third factor that both karma and dharma must wait upon, it is that of *right-timing* for setting in motion the processes of reincarnation. The 'right time' occurs when circumstances on earth accord with the karmic pattern of an individual. These bonds are conjoined with related patterns of others, and with growth-opportunities for qualifications that the Soul must now develop. These several strands weave the bondage of an incarnation.

The Incredible Undertaking

Before thinking of the method by which reincarnation proceeds, it will be of value first to consider certain general aims of this incredible undertaking. If we assume that the immortal Self is the basic spiritual center—the permanent seat of intelligence from which all venturing into incarnations goes forth and returns—the evolutionary purpose attained is that, through the discipline of limitation, exactness and precision is educed in developing life's mastery of forces and form. Through harsh impacts on the material form, comprehension grows, and with it skills are evolved; refinement and excellence follow, and through these the immortal Self increasingly inspires and guides the efforts of its mortal counterpart as the person co-operates in unfolding latent powers. Life after life, these ties that bind mortal and immortal Selfhood, are strengthened. With this growth, Soul-power at last becomes dominant in the reincarnated person. He is then able to subject his animal propensities to the more permanent aims of the Soul. Thus begins the resurrection from 'death' to immortality.

One of the greater expansions of awareness that accompany a comprehension of the law of reincarnation, is a growing identity in daily life with the immortal Self. This means the assumption of an inner point of view, as though through immortal eyes, one grasps the significance of events and relationships, and in discriminating between real and unreal values. This changing standard of values results in the permanent ones taking precedence over the transitory, in determining one's action, thus marking a change in the quality and character of daily living.

One's total pattern of individual karma determines the location, conditions, and the initial course that leads into renewal of life on earth. However, the soul of man is fundamentally endowed with a freedom of will. This is the freedom to delay or hasten one's evolution. One can slow-down progress by corrupting one's surroundings irresponsibly. Or, one can use every opportunity for growth to best advantage, and thus move onward more swiftly. One can be continually alert to the deeper realities, or one can merely idle away one's time in pleasant preoccupations. But whether opportunities are recognized and used, or whether limitations reduce one to smouldering inertia, and rebellion, depends upon Soul-recollection as to: "Who am I?" "Why am I here?" "What is the purpose of life?" The freedom gained with knowing the answers is attained only in the Soul, by the Soul. All other areas of freedom, so-called, are inevitably circumscribed by the automaticity of Nature, and the law of karma, therefore cannot be freedom in its true sense. As man's intelligence and spiritual life develop, he becomes increasingly co-operative with Nature's laws, and guidance by the Soul. Mortal and immortal man united, begin influencing, by remote control, the path ahead, thereby shortening the 'cycle of necessity'. The experience of freedom becomes identified with obedience, and from there on, growth is swifter toward ultimate freedom.

The New Mental Vehicle

The return to embodiment in material form commences in the mental world, with activation of the seed-atom of mental matter, that encloses and holds permanently the total mental ability so far developed by the reincarnating Self. A completely new mental body will coagulate around this seed, as a kind of embryo that can respond exactly to the vibratory capacities that have been brought from past lifetimes. Nothing new is added at this point, nothing has been lost. All possibilities are present in seed form, and the mental body will respond in the same manner, to the same extent that it did before, in similar experiences. The Soul that is evoking this new mental form will be limited by it, without direct recollection of past lives. But the new vehicle has the potential of memory through instinct, and when experiencing circumstances that arouse Soul-memory.

The reincarnating Self re-awakens mental capacities insofar as karmic fate in the new physical incarnation permits, particularly with respect to the inheritance of brain endowment. Generally the inheritance does not demand one's full latent abilities. Frequently a person may experience in some mysterious manner that he 'knows' more than he actually has learned. One seems at times to be able to out-think one's brain ability. The mental body, by association of ideas, reawakens latent knowledge, and furnishes additional content to what is being only partially learned through present brain capacity. This queer experience is observable, especially in elderly people whose brain activity has slowed down, or become faulty, yet whose mental alertness remains fully active. In youth and maturity, the mental body sometimes recovers its past capacities much more rapidly than the physical brain develops. In experiences where the brain is damaged yet recovers, the mental body will restore gaps in the brain storage that may have been damaged or lost. A discerning study of this dual unfoldment of the inner mental body and its outer brain compartment, offers extraordinary features, I believe, for investigation.

A New-Old Astral Body

Simultaneously, with the formation of the mental body, there occurs the activation in the astral permanent seed-atom and the collection by magnetic attraction, of an astral embryo. Again, the astral birth is a new creation that embodies in potentiality, all desiring and feeling that was experienced in previous incarnations. The qualities, the tendencies for good and evil, for pain and pleasure, sorrow and happiness, all are present, but their actual awakening will await karmic conditions, and the response of the reincarnating self to his new heredity, environment and demands made by life. The devachanic and higher spiritual influences still linger about the returning Soul. But awaiting him at the astral level is the formidable harvest of the past denoted by Buddhists as *Skandhas*— the units of desire-forms created by past indulgences in desires and sensations. These are bundles of appetites, feelings and passions, that merge into the growing personality. They are usually adverse to the Soul's direction into the future. Although skandhas are only latent at birth, as soon as the baby is born it begins to attract forcefully the astral matter that is appropriate to its skandhas. Very much now depends on environment and education, as to what kind of individual can develop from this milieu.

The Physical Body

The path of reincarnation now takes its most decisive turn. The forthcoming physical limitation is preceded by the formation of an ethereal pattern, or mould, for the embryo of the physical vehicle to be created. When the physical permanent seed-atom is activated, all physical atoms that are in the magnetic field, are drawn toward the nucleus of the embryo, the shield of the etheric double acting as a sieve, ruling out what is blocked by past karma. This etheric double of the physical body is moulded in accordance with the forces of karma and of dharma, direct influences from the past and future. These two streams mark the destiny that is unfolding for good or ill. The marvelous fact that all forces streaming from such remote origins can meet so precisely in their time orbit, is itself a miracle of life, demonstrating on a human scale, the universal order that prevails throughout all worlds. The Soul, having departed from devachan, has quietly fallen asleep, or sunk into an unconscious state, as veil after veil of mental, astral, and physical materiality focuses it into steadily diminishing horizons. What happens now is no less a miracle: the etheric matrix within which the baby's physical body is being assembled, acts as a living blueprint that summarizes all past stages of physical evolution and provides with exactitude, the limitations of physical capacities and facilities in the new body.

The Heritage

Meanwhile, karmic links have determined the human heritage and environment that are propitious. The Soul is automatically drawn to parents who are present on earth, whose ties with it, established in past life-relationships, make possible the continuation of experience in a new frame of relationship. The inevitability of return to the same group does not always follow. The Soul's dharma may dictate an entirely different experience at any point. Another orbit may be established with the new incarnation; and the Soul may be born to parents who—relatively speaking—are spiritual strangers to it.

There is a sacred beauty about the spiritual appointment that is entailed in normal and natural parenthood. It provides a common ground upon which the creative God-power in two human beings, father and mother, unite with the forces of an evolving immortal Soul in mutual creation. Usually normal womanhood is more sensitively aware of the transcendent influences connected with pregnancy, perhaps because hers is the greater responsibility. But both parents are profoundly involved in this engagement with destiny.

Determining the Parentage

The lines of attraction to the parents from the Soul about to be born to them, are established in various ways, depending upon unique circumstances. In more evolved societies, these circumstances are usually strong karmic links, or opportunities offered by the parentage to the returning soul for specialized development through the connection. With primitive people, sacred observations regarding child-bearing offer interesting occult information upon the subject of rebirth and parentage. Their customs result from age-old natural approaches. Sometimes their mythologies represent tried and true memories of Nature's processes. An interesting example is provided by certain Aboriginal people of Australia. Among some tribes, the mythology of birth is linked with a 'Dreamtime' agreement that is literally an appointment between a reincarnating soul and the parents who are to give it a physical body. The belief is held by some, that children are not born merely of sexual intercourse, but by means of the parents, or of one parent's going into the "dreaming", or into the bush, and contacting the soul who wants reincarnation through them.* The belief is that only through such an appointment does pregnancy become possible. Among these people in primitive times, such was the natural course by which karmic attraction resulted in true birth. However, throughout the long course of human evolution, karmic attraction has continued to bear the Soul to true birth, taking place in natural ways that are just as definite as the older practices, though happening more obscurely today. The contacts now are unconscious and more subtle. The Soul perhaps is still in devachan, and not in any astral or etheric contact, as it was with primitive people.

*"The Australian Aborigines", A. P. Elkin, pp. 153, 193.

The Elemental Builder

In the stages of conception, the immortal Self is not present; nor in the early stages of fetal growth in the mother's womb; although there is usually a higher spiritual rapport between the Soul of the child and that of the mother, throughout the pregnancy period. The actual development of the infant body in the womb takes place in strict accordance with the etheric pattern that was formed upon the arrival of the karmic and other forces. This proceeding is under the direction of an 'ethereal presence', sometimes known as the *body-elemental*, or 'body-deva'. This elemental creature is an intelligent unit of consciousness that remains with the person throughout his incarnation in that particular physical body. Its first and only duty is the care of the body, urging its wants, and guarding the necessary changes of pace: rest and sleep, hunger and sustenance, and all regular movements of the body, all natural functions, such as breathing and blood circulation, digestion and excretion. During pregnancy the body-elemental presides over the selecting and arranging of atoms and molecules made available for the growth and development of physical tissue and organs. The reincarnating Soul is yet unaware of all this work of Nature. It is normally in the sleep stage into which it passed on its departure from devachan.

Nepenthe

With the arrival of the Soul within its etheric form or vehicle, the full veil of forgetfulness—the curtain of 'Nepenthe' is drawn. The reincarnating Self will henceforth be within the confines of birth and death, entirely shut off from both past and future, except through awakened memory. So far as reality for it is concerned, it will have as channels of information only the five senses. There exists however, the passageway between the higher and lower self, across which Soul-memory and the higher mind can be awakened, and spiritual intuition occur. This is the *Antahkarana* referred to on the next page.

Physical Birth

As the time for birth becomes imminent, the Soul draws near, but hardly is aware on the physical plane as to what is taking place. It has little or no control over its new vehicle. For the most part, the elemental is almost entirely in charge. It is said that babies are born 'trailing clouds of glory',* and this is probably due to the strange influences of devachan that seem to cling to some of them, reflected in their eyes and general countenance. Devachan is much more in their consciousness than any attraction to the physical plane at this time. Babies that are born under unfortunate circumstances are often fully dominated by the elemental, due to their suffering and frustrations. When the infant is obstreperous and unnaturally disturbed, this is certainly the case. The first few years of infancy and childhood are difficult times for the Soul, particularly if the reincarnation happens to be a painful one, or if birth takes place in a new Race, or in the opposite sex from that of a series of previous lifetimes. Memory in such cases, is not as helpful as it is where the individual returns to his racial, national and family group. However, in any case, family love and an orderly home and school-life aid the growing child's adaptation to its new heredity and environment. Resulting discipline guides growth into the destined pattern.

Ever Truer Harvesting

Each incarnation becomes more highly specialized as more permanent growth takes place in the service of others, and of life, and of the world. Accomplishment on a

*From "Ode to the Intimations of Immortality" - from William Wordsworth (1770-1850) "Recollections of Early Childhood."

world scale becomes the larger aim of the incarnation. Very often at this stage the single incarnation is one of a series in which the aim is not fully attainable in a single lifetime. For not only must complex capabilities be developed, but the full power of the Soul can only be brought to bear in particular phases, as the larger unfoldment takes place.

Great accomplishment in one direction does not necessarily mean that equal ability is attained in all directions. Great leaders of humanity are often shown to be defective in certain aspects of their nature. When specialization has reached its culmination in an incarnation of highest all round achievement, the aim changes, and another incarnation may commence in a new direction entirely foreign to the previous one. This altered direction will mean difficulty and spiritual trials for the person who is inwardly aware of abilities that have no outlet for expression in this new direction. Incapacity, and failure are often glaring and dismaying. The demands for patience and accompanying virtues, become monumental.

But nothing has been lost, the full power of the Soul will blossom once more in the new specialization. Meanwhile, latent powers from the archetypal Self are awakening. As these come into action, the archetypal Self begins to govern the immortal Man, and the mortal person is the humble, joyful servant of the inner splendor and glory of both of his inner selves. The three are not separate, but *three selves in one*.

Gateway to Freedom

It is because purpose is known in the 'land of the Gods'—the paradise of the Soul between incarnations—that the individual Soul can voluntarily and happily take on the 'coats of skin' that imprison him for a season in the exile of mortal personality. However, there is the 'escape' roadway that has been mentioned, the mysterious passageway or channel between the higher and lower aspects of the Self, that can be cultivated, thus facilitating communication between the higher and lower levels of the Self. This instrumentality which can almost be thought of as an organ of the mind, has been recognized in occult philosophy by the name *Antahkarana**. A serious student of reincarnation will appreciate the enormous value of knowledge about this specific connection between the Soul and the personality. With it, he will be helped in unifying himself during the period of darkness in physical incarnation.

With this general outlook, it becomes clear that whatever befalls us in the way of limitations, the situation can be advantageous to the Soul. With a positive creative outlook and attitude, a greater soul-harvest is reaped, whatever the limitations happen to be.

*Ref. Glossary

11

THROUGH IMMORTAL EYES

A deeper appreciation of the Supreme Good can be experienced with each contemplation of the grand cycle of reincarnation's rhythm. With the fresh breezes that blow from immortal heights in the individual, there stirs a revolt from the ancient autocracy of the possessive, thirsting animal-nature in man. Self-revolution necessarily arises with entrainment in the cosmic circuits of consciousness. As the self-sphere grows larger, lesser shells must splinter. The real revolution today is happening interior-ally, in the mind and heart of the individual; the revolt is within the walled fortress of mortality. Those pocket-revolts that have surfaced visibly against restricting customs and conventions, against mental, spiritual and psychic barriers of uniformity, have their significances; yet they are as minor whirlpools upon the surface of a tidal flood that is lifting the universal outlook to another level of realizing life more fully. Such an estimate of the world situation requires viewing matters from the standpoint of the reincarnationist—through eyes that can glance to the wider horizons of immortality.

From a Reincarnationist Viewpoint

Today, there is a spreading involvement and commitment of interest in occultism as an approach to realizing extraordinary possibilities that life may hold for the individual. The advance in perceptivity is qualitative; it is more than superficial curiosity. Modern explorers of man's invisible nature are as pioneers who are ignorant of dangers, but who strike out for freedom, hoping to find new lands of promise. What they are discovering is that the physical body and person are shells of consciousness that can be broken through into wider consciousness—strange, sometimes fearful, yet alluring. They are finding that the life found outside of objective consciousness, means enlargement of life inside it. The wise ones learn that the true way to move *out*, is *through* the shells within.

The reincarnationist need not await death's release to mount the barricades of mortality. He can do so now, and gaze upon the entire modern scene with another kind of vision, from a loftier standpoint, that changes everything. The main highway to supreme knowing is before him, plainly marked by eternal principles: *Life is a total unity; Evolution is universal; Reincarnation's cycles are wheels of growth; Karma equilibrizes all motion.* Those who travel the highway with intelligence and integrity, will find at length, faith in the Law; the good life of right beliefs and right action. They move toward the heights. Those who wander aimlessly in the mental wilderness, or in the wastelands of desire and satiation, through lifetimes, will be delayed in desolation and further confinement.

The reincarnationist knows that the harvest of today's life is tomorrow's heritage. It is a sobering realization that no break is possible between cause and effect. All bondage originates in uncompleted circuits of action and reaction. If they are not pursued to fulfilled equilibrium, the uncompleted cycles exist immortally. Everyone returns in due season to the unresolved situation. Yet freedom to tread the higher road does not wait upon the completion of every circuit. The cycles themselves *are* the road; obeying the law of harmony, all are completed finally. The whole universe is in motion in all stages of return to an eternal harmony that includes all discords.

Pollution of the Shared Worlds

Rightly there is great concern among thoughtful people with respect to environmental pollution, and with the depletion of natural resources through uncaring extravagant usage. The various destructive forms of ecological damage are multiplying. But the shared sphere is much greater than the physical earth; the human environment, according to the reincarnationist, includes the astral world of feelings, and the mental world of thoughts. These are actual worlds, indeed being the afterlife worlds into which all of us return at death. Pollution of the physical planet begins in the invisible worlds. Man, while physically incarnated, thinks and feels *before* he acts. His gross thoughts and desires pollute first the mental and astral worlds before the actions are carried out in the physical plane. All physical disorder has its roots in the slothful mind, together with impulsive desiring, and careless irresponsible action. Pollution is multiplied by antiunity thinking, and by the craving for possessions to hold in secure exclusiveness. As physical resources dwindle, and population demands grow, the increasing mental and astral selfishness will become as physical time-bombs that can be de-fused only by a rapidly expanding sense of individual responsibility for the whole shared sphere. Such a swift growth might become possible with the universal spread of the knowledge of reincarnation and the karmic inheritance by everyone of exactly the effects of all that one has done and left undone. Obviously, at this point in evolution, a tremendous opportunity exists for man to leap ahead in spiritual unfoldment through recognizing and acting upon the responsibility we all share in serving the whole of life—on the physical as well as other levels.

Need for Knowledge

It has become very noticeable in recent decades that there has been the extraordinary increased interest in occultism. To the reincarnationist, this may be a healthy trend, because it arouses interest in that side of Nature, the pursuit of which reveals that man survives the death of his physical body. This kind of knowledge has been left out of the educational processes. Since there is no orderly approach to the occult domain, with proper precautions, it has had a more or less disorderly unveiling. Information arrives from various directions, with fraud and delusion adding to the confusion. Misguided foraging amidst the quagmires of occultism is dangerous, and can bring tragic results. Moreover, when motivated by exploitative intentions, occult knowledge can become handmaiden to a lawless, irresponsible cultivation of sensational experiences and insights—and what is more dangerous, the release of occult powers and their misuse.

But the interest in the occult will go on, and undoubtedly increase. It is not a passing phase. Man's education as to his real nature must proceed swiftly, if not through the organized educational system, then willy-nilly under the pressure of events, through whatever means exist. How can a free society that releases cosmic power in the physical world, hope to survive, if it is not disciplined by a knowledge of cosmic principles that control the universe? The principles of universal order that govern the occult world, or hidden side of Nature, must be given recognition if the present swiftening course toward world catastrophe is to be changed. A nuclear world war can destroy physical humanity; but not the immortal souls that will return to the sorrow and horror of reconstructing what remains. The shallows of occultism that are involved with astral and etheric phenomena, magical effects, clairvoyance, astral projection, and other sensationalized occult arts, must be more accurately perceived as holding an inferior position in the larger perspectives of universal principles from which stem the laws of Nature. Certain of the greater realities have been dealt with in this book, but what has been said is incomplete if further mention is not made of the dangers that are rife in that playground of the desire nature of man—the astral plane. The reincarnationist has some comprehension of the astral sub-planes, from densest to the most ethereal levels. He sees readily how lust, greed, and selfishness, can quickly draw one into satanic practices that can lead to ultimate evil. The dangers are not to be taken lightly. On the astral plane are not only angels of goodness, mercy and light, but demons of darkness, elemental and anti-human. Evolution is a two-way stream plunging downward into the depths of materiality, as well as rising upward to kingdoms above. In between are the playful, irresponsible elemental entities, with a huge capacity for deluding the unwary. The whole astral domain is delusive, being obedient to the tidal movements of emotional forces. All of these matters should be illuminated with reliable knowledge, and taught by those who seek only to lift the curtains that enclose man in his prison of mortality.

The Permissive Age

Today's permissiveness is popularizing the fundamental togetherness of humanity. We've had many permissive ages; those of war and horror, for example, ages of permissive religious persecution; modern permissiveness of commercial and industrial exploitation; and eras of permissive stratification of humanity, with unconscionable social schemes. But today's order of permissiveness is of another kind. It is seeking freer access to the realities of psychic realms; the realities of personal togetherness, of mental, emotional and physical sharing with one another; of finding the security of unity; of permitting others to express themselves in a mutual discovery of what is over the next barrier of self.

Many curious investigators are opening fields that are strange to them, and that hold grave dangers for the unwary. Exploring new worlds, without guidance, individuals get lost. Sometimes in occultism, so-called "guides" that receive recognition as such, mis-guide, opening the way to disaster. But in the cycles of reincarnation, no individual in the struggle upwards loses anything. He inherits upon his return, the fruits of his having lived in, and contributed to, this time; to his having served, unconsciously though it may have been, in the human advancement that was attained. Any price he may have paid returns as beneficent karma in a new age. The mistakes made, karma rectifies in the fate of individuals and groups. The violent and vicious ones return to their own doom to repeat unlearned lessons. There need be no fear of the pioneering that is taking place. Nor should we, out of anxiety for ourselves and way of life, visit persecution upon those who see differently and intend to live as they think is right, so long as their way does not deny the right of others to find their own way. Every individual will awaken in time to his weaknesses, as well as his inherent powers. Meanwhile, the permissiveness surrounding us is registering and weighing the actual levels of moral, social and spiritual evolution attained by humanity.

The Drug Scene

From the reincarnation point of view, a reminder to the drug addict (which includes the alcoholic) is that, in addition to the harm done to the physical body, there is damage to the etheric vehicle. Since this is perpetrated while on earth, the condition will show up even more disastrously after the death of the physical body. One is to be reminded also that addiction brings the prospect of a reincarnation into conditions that present the same compulsive situation, karmically worsened. One can sink into ugliness and cruelty, violence, filth and negative indolence, all of which are magnets that attract the worst elements around one who indulges in conditions that invite such influences. Permitting the possession of one's vehicles by such entities, places the bodies beyond control of the sovereign Self. The insidious danger of drug addiction is this inviting of invisible entities to assume dominant control of oneself. Without being aware of it, the addict is easily and swiftly conveyed beyond depths with which he can cope.

Sex Confusion

The dawn of true sex equality awaits a general recognition and acceptance of the reincarnationist outlook, because from that standpoint, the chauvinist male and female attitudes will disappear in an illumined perception of the co-equality of the sexes. The world is waiting for that sunrise. Too long has the lordly male, striding along his high road, been conscious that his feminine mate 'rightly' travels at a somewhat subordinate level. In the light of reincarnation, one sees that inevitably tomorrow, or the day after, the high road and the low road will be reversed for everyone. That will be the day of true realization of the equal value of both sexes. The basic fact of the sex difference is that there are actually two, and only two, entirely different kinds of human beings on earth—two different races: male and female, they are counterparts of each other. Moreover, these two manifestations of entirely different natures are channeling the two positive-negative cosmic forces or, if you will, masculine-feminine, that hold the universe together in a balanced harmony. The individual Soul of man, reincarnating in first one, then the other kind of human being, is rounding out the evolution of his individual immortal Self. This Self, or Soul, is dual-sexed—neither masculine nor feminine, but both— that is to say 'androgynous'. Each individual, man or woman, is both masculine-feminine in his spiritual nature. Born in one sex, the Soul experiences emphasis upon one of the two cosmic forces playing through it. In a later incarnation, in the opposite sex, there will be emphasis upon the alternative force. Yet, the immortal Soul, being dual-powered, is manifesting both cosmic forces. When one is major, the other is minor, and vice versa. As this profound truth becomes more thoroughly digested, the powers of both sexes will be properly evaluated.

At present, ignorance of reincarnation and the Soul's balancing growth, is contributing to the prevailing confusion. Individuals who have had a series of several lifetimes experiencing the masculine privileges, and now find themselves in female bodies, naturally have difficult adjustments to make—which is equally true for the other sex. But these difficulties are lessened somewhat in our permissive age of sex-exploration with its various diversions, deviations, and transvestite experiences, which are commonly publicized today. The conditions of sex abnormality are recognized, and are receiving wider general acceptance, even though the basic cause (cyclic reincarnation) is not yet in view. The commercialization of complex sex situations by the entertainment industry is dramatizing, therefore spreading an awareness of these problems and their solutions. But a basic insight would be attained with a knowledge of the whole cycle of reincarnation.

The Co-Equal Way

The beautiful truth underlying co-equality of the sexes has not been fully elicited from the biblical story of Creation. When God said: (Genesis) "Let us make man in our image, after our likeness", and He acted, ". . . male and female created he them". The point that seems to have been missed is that if the dual humanity of masculine and feminine beings is to become a balanced harmony, thereby attaining a "likeness of God" on earth, the likeness will have been achieved as a harmonious man-woman unity. How long will such an evolution require? Yet the ideal has been approached in some instances of truly creative love-marriages and this is why they remain the happiest dream imaginable. The masculine-feminine union points the way to the spiritual goal of Man. Notably, reincarnation promises an ultimate attainment of this 'impossible dream' by its revelation of the technical means by which all necessary qualities are evoked from the latent powers of the Soul. Man experiences first one-half of his divine nature, in a love-relationship with another human being, who symbolically represents his Soul; and then the other half, similarly, until the transformation has been perfectly wrought of individually-sexed human beings evolved at length into androgynous Godhood. The sex-bliss that so beguiles modern people, is in actuality a reminder of the individual's incompleteness. Sex faintly reflects the God-bliss that lies ahead. But it is a faint reminder, and—significantly—has a peculiar note of sadness and loneliness that at times accompanies sex indulgence, particularly when it is without love. This experience is further testimony to the profound meaning revealed in man's sexual nature. The animal deprived of love is a creature without Soul-experience; the anticipated sex-bliss does not culminate in illumined joy and deep peace; it ends in empty desolation. Violent sex savagery, enslavement to importunity and other forms of sex abuse, are indulgences dominated by the animal man, and will be corrected karmically through pain and sorrow in experience that will awaken one at last to the real nature of this fiery power, so central to man's nature.

The spiritual value of the sex alternation in a series of lifetimes is obvious to the reincarnationist observer. The mortal human being is ever hoping for an ideal relationship with someone in whom can be experienced (even though unconsciously) the beauteous other half of himself or herself—the immortal Soul. If the individual is masculine, the Soul-dream is represented in his feminine partner. Conversely, the Soul-image for the woman, is sought in her masculine counterpart. Seeking an ideal mate, the woman looks for her other half, which actually exists in higher worlds, as has been explained. She will find—she hopes—the archetypal Self reflected in the qualities of the man she loves. Everyone perforce, seeks the real in the unreal. The actual "marriage made in heaven" is that of the Soul with its eternal Spirit, the union in paradise, that precedes the cosmic union of Self with God. This transcension is reflected on earth in the love union that mutually joins two individuals in an expression of unitedness with their immortal Souls. Thus the influence of each human being upon the other is opposite and vital. This counter-play of forces, masculine and feminine, act as a self-regulating system in advancing the evolution of the spiritual nature of both individuals.

Seeking the 'ideal' in a mate, people involve themselves in matrimonial conjugation with its huge and multiplying problems. These bring both joys and sorrows, along with whatever blissful or disagreeable conditions the marriage relationship might turn into. Each benefits unknowingly from the influences of the other, whatever abrasions or upliftments occur. Each is being schooled by the intimate association with the other. The reincarnationist can only view with deep and understanding sympathy, the futility of the mad sex scramble of men and women today who search for a mythical happiness that does not take into account the spiritual meaning of the masculine-feminine union, as revealed by a knowledge of the Soul's growth through reincarnation.

Trend to Violence

One notices everywhere, that there is a thinning substratum of contented individuals, those who accept with patience and goodwill their condition in life, however insufferable.

Except for a rare few, people in general apparently believe that life is treating them unfairly; that they are embattled by modern circumstances, and are being exploited unjustly. The only answer, it seems is to strike back violently. There are many causes why this is so, but there is a deeper underlying root-cause that is not receiving undivided attention.

In the industrialized nations where communication is becoming universal through visualized news and entertainment, crime and violence is the constant fare. Some psychologists advise that the violence appearing in all the media acts as an outlet for the pent-up resentments, and that without such release there would be even more explosive and tragic physical acts of violence. In other words, by producing and viewing fictional violence, we are avoiding further acts of actual violence.

To the reincarnationist, this answer reveals one of the more dismal aspects of today's unawareness of man's inner nature. The frightening release of animality that is surfacing, is directly triggered by the endless visualization of vice, violence and indulgences of the lower nature. There are few forces of enlightenment to neutralize effectively this trend. It properly lies in the field of education.

But the educational impacts that have widest influence, particularly upon the younger children, are being delivered in the home through television, and other visually delineated ways of modern life. Thus the animal nature in the young is being enticed forth—by every cunning device that can be engineered to arouse it. The unreal qualities of this world are made to appear the real. Life's values are distorted visually. It is not difficult to see that such training prepares youth to resort to violence when it cannot otherwise gain its way. A common news event on television has been the sight of university students in protest riots. They give witness of the ancient truth that hatred is the downpour that answers hating; violence only can result. What a transformation would occur were we taught from childhood the occult facts of life, together with a cultivation of faith in the lawful nature of the universe, and based upon this foundation, were there induced a new spiritual self-reliance and sense of responsibility. The dominant keynote in today's trend to violence is the visualization of violence repeated endlessly. Among those who are violence-inclined, thoughtforms are created that are vitalized with emotional content, and made virulent with repetition. With the usage that modern civilization is making of its communication miracles, we could be educating reincarnated barbarians. The world receives what it merits. There is no closing of the door of reincarnation, nor of circumventing karma.

Population Growth

A question often addressed to reincarnationists is that of the phenomenal population growth in modern times. Non-reincarnationists have pointed to the mounting population within a few centuries, as being irreconcilable with the theory of reincarnation, because, as they point out, if people are reincarnating with only brief periods between lives, and if no new Souls are being born, then where do all these people come from, who are born on earth today? They were not here 200 years ago, nor, according to present historians, were such large numbers here in earlier times. The population of the world, they repeat, has always been very much smaller than it is today. If reincarnation were true, they argue, how could there be such an enormous increase in population in such a short span of time?

The confusion stems directly from ignoring the occult nature of man. The normal cycle of reincarnation is much longer than is usually realized. The after-worlds that are traversed, following the death of the physical body, are numerous and time-consuming. This accounts for a distribution of billions of egos that are not appearing on earth at any given time, because the span of absence from the physical world is far greater than that of any persons' lifetime here on earth. This means that there are many more reincarnating egos in our Life-wave than are present at any time. Even the four billion people that are crowding the planet today, approximate only a small percentage of those who are said to be evolving in our earth-scheme. In any case, Space within extends to infinity in higher dimensions of consciousness; and it is consciousness that is evolving. Except on the physical plane, Space offers no problem, and in higher dimensions of consciousness Time has no existence as we know it.

Reincarnation and Materialism

The theme of this book renders reincarnation a rational outlook. Its intellectual ancestry lifts it beyond mere superstition. It is anti-materialistic, since the cycle of the reincarnating Self begins with and ends in the Soul's immortal base. The growth of the Soul, through reincarnation, fulfills its destiny in union with the Source of All.

The wisdom innate in the knowledge of reincarnation utterly refutes the intellectual anchorage to materiality—for example, the supposition that strings of molecules can produce life. Only the hardiest superstition of the material mind could suppose that life, beginning in that way, could evolve intelligence that ultimately can perform the immortal works of the Soul. From the reincarnationist point of view, life precedes form, and form can only channel the life that is already present. Intelligence is *evoked*—not evolved—as the channel becomes clearer. Moreover, physical bodies are obviously composites of elements that cannot hold together without the presence of the indwelling sovereign Self which is not subject to death. The fact of its withdrawal at the time the physical body dies, is plainly shown by the process of physical decomposition that commences at that instant. The massive collection of matter that is one's physical body, is sustained as a unity only as long as the Self is present. It is the nature of the body's multitudinous constituents that each will go its own way, if released from the imposed *will to unity*. The body, being vulnerable to destructive agents that are ever-ready to break apart its unity, is able nevertheless, to maintain its functional form because of the ruling power of the dweller within. Distinct from matter is this organizer of matter's wayward tendencies, coercing all into the disciplined order of the body. The Organizer is a unity of will, intelligence, and creative power. This spiritual Self commands its own ancient wisdom of Nature's laws, the primeval knowledge of a consciousness, that once evolved in the rocks, enduring eons of fire, wind and tidal floods; this Self was once the consciousness in the minerals become precious stones, in the grasses evolved into sequoias, in the animals that have become man, and in humanity that responds directly to the indwelling, eternal God-Self. The Self is the uniter, the knower, who has been present all the while, awakening cosmic memory. Mortal man, then, is linked to his immortal knowing and beyond, to the eternal Knower. If the three remain together consciously the sense of direction can never be lost; and all situations, relationships and choices can be seen and judged through 'immortal eyes'. Plainly, this position is the antithesis of materialism. Rather than being rooted in materialism, the reincarnationist viewpoint flows from a deepening penetration into the far-ranges of occultism and the non-material Reality.

The following are a few of the more commonly asked questions about reincarnation.

Can you prove reincarnation? See Appendix "A". No proofs can be offered that meet laboratory standards of repeatable exactitude. Neither can the existence of the Soul be incontrovertably substantiated by scientific methods. Love is a reality experienced consciously by practically everyone, yet love is beyond the reach of scientific proof. Similarly, reincarnation cannot be proved by material, exact science. One becomes convinced of inner realities only through memory of one form or another.

Is not reincarnation unjust? The question has been asked: "Why am I made to pay for something done by somebody else?" (In other words, why should my personality in this life pay the karma of a person who lived in the past?) This question could be asked only by those who are so completely identified with their present mortal personality that it is impossible for them to think of the Self as being in another body of another race and a different time. As long as we believe that we are no more than what we see in the mirror each day, the gap between lifetimes will completely obliterate any links between succeeding personalities. Hence, it might well be said by any one of them that the karma of "somebody else" is being inherited.

The Bible records this question being asked of Jesus, when he healed the blind man: "Who did sin, this man, or his parents, that he was born blind?"*—The question implies that all of them believed in reincarnation, for if a man is *born* blind, how could he have committed the sin except in a previous lifetime? Jesus' answer is even more illuminating, for he said: "Neither hath this man sinned, nor his parents, but that the works of God should be made manifest in him."** The answer is illuminating if one realizes that the Soul is evolving divine potentials, growing into perfect Godhood, through incarnations wherein errors are made and corrected by the universal law of karma. Thus, in the larger perspective, the workings are beneficent, the "Works of God" are being made "manifest in him". From the reincarnationist point of view, there can be no injustice in the balancing of karmic scales, life after life.

Why is there so much contradictory information regarding reincarnation? Dissimilar and contradictory versions are to be expected, regarding a journey so completely individual as is the reincarnation trip. If fifty people were to get on a bus at the same point, and disembark together at another point, no two individuals would render the same account of what they saw, felt and thought. The basic facts, of course, would all be the same: such as the points of boarding, and of disembarkation, and the fact that the journey did take place—all could agree upon these essential facts. But the points of interest, the comforts and discomforts, the delights and novelties, would be matters of personal response. If we compare this bus trip to a group of people reincarnating, everyone would have to agree that there was certainly a point of death, and a journeying inwardly; and that obviously they have arrived here, reborn. But, would any two people agree as to exactly what happened, what they saw, and what they thought? In fact, would anyone remember any of it?

*John 9:2
**Ibid 9:3

People just do not see the same things, or if they do, they interpret differently what they see.

What is needed is a natural reminder of basic truths to aid their comprehension of what is seen and experienced—some structure that is simple, clear and reasonable, that will assist the recognition of memories when these do appear. Such a mnemonic is the Ancient Wisdom that has been in the world for ages of time, and is being restated in modern times by Theosophy and kindred pursuits of spiritual wisdom. Contradictory versions are found here also. Consequently, one must arrive at one's own understanding of these matters, assisted by the discoveries of explorers in these fields.

Does reincarnation throw light upon the problem of Good and Evil? The Evolution of life began visibly upon this earth in the mineral kingdom. But life's original Source lies beyond the subtlest realms of the conceivable domain. Before *evolution* commences in the mineral kingdom, there is a preceding *involution* of life down into matter—an involvement that moves toward life's nadir in densest physical matter. This aim indicates that there are two streams of life: (a) the tidal flow *into* matter, designated involution, that identifies life with materiality in ever denser forms; and (b) the growth of consciousness up out of dense matter, the growth that is recognized as life's evolution. The two opposite streams give rise to friction. There are collisions, obstructions and fragmentations brought about by their juxtaposed currents. Moving in diametrically opposite directions, yet attracted by one another, as are positive by negative forces, the resulting conflicts and general disharmony, in the long run, are obstructive to the intended progress. The abrasive factor produces strength through opposition. Each side then experiences through the opposing side a retarding of its growth. The retarding agent is denoted as 'evil'.

It may be useful to realize that those forces that are

'evil' for one stream, are 'good' for the other. What assists the stream flowing into denser matter, is evil for the stream evolving out of matter. Humanity is in the *evolutionary* stream. Man necessarily, and rightly, views every influence of forces aimed downward into brutishness, into identity with matter and materiality as 'evil'. The evolution of humanity's consciousness is advancing through refinement toward unity and freedom from imprisonment in material forms. All that assists progress in this direction is 'good'.

When did reincarnation begin? In the human being, reincarnation began eons ago, when the *causal body* was formed, at the time of human *individualization*. This technical phrasing indicates that a graduation took place into the human kingdom from the animal kingdom during the course of evolution. At that moment, for each individual, the forming of a so-called causal body provides a permanent vehicle for an immortal Soul to evolve through physical incarnation. From then on, the individual reincarnates as a human being. Men and women of today have had hundreds of lifetimes on earth, to have evolved the high levels of intelligence and moral consciousness of those who are capable of leading the world struggle against ignorance, and the anti-human behavior that threatens destruction to life on earth.

When will it end? Involuntary reincarnation ends with the balancing of all cycles of karma. When the karmic indebtedness has achieved equilibrium through wise living, no forces remain that can draw the reincarnating self again into limitation. Life's lessons will have been learned, and the Soul's growth will have reached its fullness, so far as this physical world is concerned. If there is any further reincarnation, it will be voluntary, and for purposes of teaching or guiding the evolution of others.

Will I be born in the opposite Sex? Generally, we reincarnate in the same sex for several lifetimes, then change to the opposite sex. This is not universally true, for a number of reasons. But as the Soul becomes more highly evolved, the alternations tend to be more frequent, because the masculine-feminine balancing of the whole nature is rapidly approaching its completion, with respect to this earth.

Why haven't I been told before of reincarnation? A strange intellectual inertia seems to beset the spread of this knowledge in the West. Those who are in positions to encourage the recognition of this principle that is so obviously operating in the lives of everyone, and with such important bearing upon the spiritual welfare of humanity, seem to give it little or no attention. Perhaps the implications of reincarnation are the real cause of its rejection. Full recognition of the idea would require an abandonment of several cherished 'fundamentals', particularly the principle that life *begins* in physical materiality. The reincarnation conception embraces the greater perspective of life's *wholeness*—both the involution into matter, as well as life's evolution out of matter. There are, however, an increasing number of writers on this subject, as well as a growing library of 'reincarnalia' (Ref. p. 146-7). Perhaps its popularization will arrive in this way. Reincarnation was formerly considered by the general public as a part of Eastern religions, but it now is accepted as applying universally, without regard to one's religion.

12

CREATIVE FORGETTING AND REMEMBERING

Creative Forgetting

Blessed among the endowments of reincarnation is the veiling of the past effectively, but not absolutely. This provision of release from the burden of memory enhances the Soul's drive forward through the experiences of a new lifetime with fresh energies, unhampered by the failures that attended the same, or similar experiences in the past. With attentive thought given to this ingenius natural arrangement, it's beneficence can be profoundly appreciated. The blotting out of physical memory makes possible an entirely new approach to the same kind of problem that has barred the progress of the soul in the past, and still remains to be fully resolved.

Let us suppose that two souls are closely linked together in one life as mother and daughter, and between them there is a strong underlying emotional antagonism that reaches painful climaxes in irreconcilable situations finally end in an unhappy separation for the remainder of their lives. In a later lifetime they are born in the same community, and in their adult lives they are drawn together as man and wife. In this new relationship they meet once again the old emotional karma, and must deal with it. But it reappears in a new relationship, free of detailed memory, while at the same time there may be an awareness of the problem that can only be solved harmoniously through love. It is a Soul problem. With a little imagination one may see how this kind of situation dealt with again and again through various incarnations, can finally flower into a new power of the Soul, an expansion of the quality of love to deal with all problems in that direction.

One can readily understand that circumstances can develop between two individuals who, through hatred, ill will, and violence, might have caused each other calamities, and even death, several times in past lifetimes. And in each new situation, karma would demand self-sacrificing service by one to the other, until the powerful cycles have been equilibrized. Looking far ahead, one might see an ultimate outcome of this difficult course, resulting in a unity of two souls with bonds of loyalty and love, in unbreakable links that will endure all divisive trials, thus rendering their unity completely dependable for work together in the future.

Creative forgetting erases all ugly scars left by painful incidents, so that eternal beauty may be revealed. The cosmic principle is simply that of supplanting a memory of failure with new vision and strength by means of death and the processes of reincarnation. The bodies that actually endured the struggles are eliminated, while the faculties blossoming from them are retained by the Soul. Each time, as the Soul returns, it moves forward with new confidence, awakened in its hidden powers and resources. We see healthy youth everywhere demonstrating this truth. The wave of youth leaps forward to fresh achievement, burying the tired wreckage of the past. After death, and the long period of devachanic contemplation and association with

pure radiances of wisdom and divine love, the Soul returning in its new infant body, arrives with life's morning-
freshness, yet pregnant with divine powers, and ready to
meet the hazards, and master the difficulties when they
arise. Such is the wonder of creative forgetting.

Creative Remembering

The new-born infant is absorbed in gaining control of its
physical vehicle and astral drives. The bright new mental
body remains quietly in a state of 'non-thought-forming'.
Meanwhile it is becoming adjusted to the new brain,
which is receiving impressions of the general surroundings and circumstances of its fresh incarnation. If the
home and family life is normally affectionate, the situation
is ideal for the returned Soul to cement his complete break
from conscious detailed memory of any physical past. The
child takes up the new life in freedom to use zestfully its
opportunities to overcome past errors. Aided by such
breaks in the cycles of time as reincarnation affords, Man,
the Immortal, evolves more swiftly towards liberation
from all limitation.

The Soul's return to earth through the veil of forgetfulness becomes, in normal childhood and youth, a voyage of
discovery, an unfolding of faculties attained in the past,
that are a great delight to recapture in new forms. There is
unhampered concentration in the new development. The
fires of adversity awaken new strength, the challenges of
defeat, new courage. Intense ecstacies and desolations
unveil truths that are simple and clear. One is not bound
by the past, or the future; the present is enough; there is
the now. The freshness and eagerness in all this, are
remindful of the Soul's freedom in its own realm. And this
is what is revealed by creative remembering: this
'seeing-eagerly' with Soul-strength, and knowing that the
kind of thinking that binds one in dark and lonely worlds,
can be left behind and below, for it is always possible to

climb to that inner altitude where one breathes again the rarer atmosphere, and gazes upon the Light that is never lost; it is always there. To be aware of this facility, is to be certain that behind the ever-changing shadows on our horizons, is the imperishable Self-sun, even now transforming the clouded edges with silvery etching. The poignancy of transient life is as a bird upon the wing: its shape and shadow are fleeting impressions, but its gift of beauty awakens memory of things immortal. All fleeting experiences are ever being transformed by the Changeless.

With the attainment of a certain evenness of life, through study, reflection, and meditation, one may begin to realize an identity with the immortal Self, and begin to reflect that joyous outlook that seems somehow to remain above the storms of life, confident of the power within, to equilibrate karmic forces. The main effort is to transform knowledge into knowing. This is done through remembering. We can know about many things, but until the essence of that knowledge has become so much a part of our nature that we live by it, we have not truly *remembered* it, we have only heard of it and therefore believe that we know it. It requires a concentration of attention and of growing into what we have learned in order for it to come alive in us as memory. When, however, one touches what is truth and there is an intuitive flash of recognition—of knowing—one can be sure that this is some part of one's memory system functioning creatively. And the recovered jewel takes its proper place in one's growing awareness. It is not enough to hear that we are immortals—we must *become* immortals in our outlook in all directions. We have almost literally to pull ourselves up by our 'spiritual bootstraps'. The conviction that we are immortally alive *now*, must be applied universally in our daily dealing with physical, emotional, mental, and spiritual problems.

An application of the reincarnation principle of memory obscuration and recollection might help us in dealing with problems of the present lifetime. The faculty of creative forgetting and remembering, might be cultivated and applied in a natural and artistic way daily, in the same manner as it operates in the larger cycle of death and rebirth. We might, for example, upon retiring at night, provide a brief period for contemplative reviewing of the day just closed, together with a meditation or a reading along inspirational lines, that will turn our attention to the reality of the inner worlds. The idea is to free the mind of mundane involvement with the unresolved situations, the inept blunders, and threats of failure—intent upon harmonizing the self before sleeping. Then upon awakening in the morning, the night having been restful, the new beginning can be given added zest if assisted by a period of meditation, wherein the inner vision is recaptured, with the sense of what we really are, and what our powers are to cope with the situations of the day ahead. This kind of practice could be developed as an art that parallels in daily life the process between lifetimes of creative forgetting and remembering.

The preceding chapters in this book have emphasized the ideas of life's unity; of the inner structure of Man's consciousness that expands in unbroken stages to union with the One Source. And above all, the book has touched on the inner structure of the universe, in that there is an Authentic Archetypal Universe, the crowning implication of which is that a Cosmic Intelligence intends the evolution of a perfect universe. Our guarantee of this reality is the fact that our tap-root of consciousness springs from this archetypal region of perfection. And finally, there is the additional assurance that there must be perfected human beings who are preceding us in evolution, who, having achieved the stages toward which we are moving, stand as ideal representatives of that which we ourselves will one day become. We can begin the search for these Adepts of the mastery of life's forces.

Within the greater horizons of the above realizations, cosmic remembering can be sought. Life can become resplendent with creative powers that are possible when we have recognized individual kingship from within. It becomes possible to rise above stressful murky conditions, and move in freedom from the violence below. The task is to attain repeatedly with definiteness, the position of immortality. We must evolve our own technique for doing this. But the foundation for any technique must ever rest upon a basic knowledge that supports it. We might gain assistance, however, in developing our own, from suggested practices of others.

Practice of Cosmic Remembering

Seek each morning some place of privacy in which to break completely the routine cycles of forces that envelop one every day. This might seem tantamount to saying "stop the world, I want to get off!" But the intent is not escapism; it is a flight *to* Reality—the removal of illusions. Having situated oneself in a position of momentary quietude, recall the invisible Light which is universal, all about us. It is the Light Eternal, the Light that created the universe. It is here now, as always. Becoming aware of this inner Light, one can focus an immensely greater concentration of it in oneself through the use of the will. A practical method for doing so can be developed. To begin with, one remembers that the universe is created from the subtlest spiritual regions, level by level downward, to the physical Solar System. The life forces of vitality and nourishment are pouring through the fourth dimension into the third, and are welling up through the center of atoms, cells and human bodies at each level. The forces are radiating outward from the center to the whole, in each system, just as the sun each day radiates energy to the whole Solar System. The powers of the Soul, and those from the Spirit beyond, appear from within ourselves through the *center of the Self*. The center is ever there; it never disappears; it is the same center at all levels, because all the levels are really different dimensions of consciousness. The position of your center in any level or dimension, is the same position, geographically, as the center in your physical body. So, from wherever you are the consciousness deepens—center by center—until it is ultimately centered in the Absolute. And even then, it is the same center in yourself. In meditation, with concentrated will, bring this universal Light down into the physical body, imagining the center as being somewhere in the region of the physical heart center. (But not *in* the heart).

You can, with the will, now send the Light shining out through the whole physical body—the trunk and the limbs, hands, feet and top of the head. With practice this will bring about a vital new radiance in the body—even relieving minor aches and pains. You may find that you can eliminate pain pills for ordinary discomforts.

With the physical body vitalized, you can cause the Light to irradiate the emotional self, through the center there. The center is the same, but at the deeper astral level. Try feeling, with the aid of the Light, a pure and selfless wave of love that is radiant, unifying, possessing nothing, shining beneficently in all directions. This practice will evolve a height of lasting happiness that is not often experienced, except in one's more inspired moments.

Now, turn the focussed attention to the mental self, and dwell deeply in the facilities of the mind. The mental self has two functions: one deals, through the brain, with material necessity and the other opens the way to God. The brain-mind is a continuous news-reel and computerizing instrument, ceaselessly storing pictures and facts. This noisy confusion can be brought to stillness—at least momentarily. This is possible by using the Light, conceiving it as shining in the mental center, serenely radiating outwardly, sweeping away all the thought-forms, and bringing about a blessed quietude. Dwell, then, in the silence. With this accomplishment, the brain-mind can be rendered reflective of the higher Self. At this moment a transition can take place: consciousness becomes elevated and centered in the immortal mind—the region oriented to the Source of All. In the higher mind, one can reach a realization of the immortal Self.

It is here that the great illumination may dawn upon one. As long as we have identified ourselves entirely with the body, the desires, and business of the mind, we have been utterly oblivious of our true nature. This identification in materiality has afforded a contentment in the life of the bodies. But as the inner consciousness begins to grow and expand, the animal nature experiences suffering. Spiritual hunger makes the world a dreary place; a restless discontentment develops, that cannot be explained; it apparently has no cause. We become aware of mysterious powers within, while without we are prisoners in material confinement. There must be relief from pressure, release from our distress. Prometheus bound to the rock of matter, is an apt allusion to our situation.

But now, with what we have learned, and with the use of meditation, as described, we may take up the daily effort that leads to knowledge, and knowledge to remembering; deeper illumination follows and meditation reaches the Soul-level. The exploration can continue onward, as one awakens deeper layers of cosmic remembering. It is possible to attain the mighty divide between the immortal and the divine Self, experiencing flashes of union with the All—from which, even though experienced only fleetingly, there flows a spiritual self-reliance and confidence in one's unique being to endure all discouragements and obstacles, ultimately dissolving them into the Unity within, by the awakened power of divine Love. Thus may the Self be realized, and remembered.

The Remembering must not be permitted to disappear. Again and again one must achieve it with ever greater firmness, until one remains steadily situated within, above the storms, and can, at will, bring down the Light into the physical world. It comes as a fresh, vital consciousness of courage and joy, a gladness to be alive and helpful, with a readiness to serve life by being what one is. The inner Light will continue to glow as long as it is radiating outwardly at all levels, mentally, emotionally, and physically. The secret is to keep the channel open at the lower levels—those of readiness to sacrifice self through giving and serving.

This transformation of the self wrought momentarily at first, through meditation attains the purpose of reincarnation, which is the awakening of cosmic memory of the identity of the transient personage with the Immortal, and then with the Eternal Self. After which, there remains only to work out cheerfully the balances of karma, however long this may take, meanwhile avoiding that thoughtless indifference which forges new links of bondage, as consciousness continues to transcend all separated states of being.

Passages to Reality

Remembering inwardly may take many different pathways, depending upon the changing circumstances. In one brief period of six weeks, while crossing the Pacific Ocean, I stood morning after morning at dawn, leaning against a foremast on the forward deck of a passenger ship, with consciousness only upon the starry constellations above, and the shoreless ocean around me, as wondrous reminders, boosting me almost instantaneously into a state of immortal consciousness, the experience of which remains as creative memory.

A number of years were spent in South India*, with meditation normally and peacefully practiced on a flat roof terrace. At other times, it was pursued more informally, such as in the daily journey by bicycle to the office, nearly a mile away. Each morning's bicycling

---

*The Theosophical Society, Adyar, Madras.

along that narrow winding path bordering the wide river, and through coconut groves, became a challenging passage of inner realization. The physical hazards of negotiating the path sharpened perceptivity, and rendered each trip a yogic performance of attention. It required hardly ten minutes. Swiftly, one's consciousness had to be released from the necessity for outer alertness, to inner union with Nature: the graceful palm trees, the golden shafts of sunlight plunging through violet mists in the grove, the plaintive cries of fishermen on the river, the jubilant call of crows and mynah birds, the glory of clouds and skies—all experienced together in a union of beauty and loveliness. But consciousness must flash onward to become an awareness that breaks free of *all* forms, merging into boundless Space with its center the radiant Will that reflects one's Archetype. In a lightning-like exposure to it, time disappears in instancy, or 'instantaneity'. From 'here' on the bicycle to 'there' in the timeless archetypal is instantaneous extension. Instantaneity is freedom in Space, omnipresence its motion. Since there is no fragment that is not of the Whole, there is no particle not linked through omnipresence. Without moving from the wheel-chair, or off the bed, or bicycle, one is everywhere. The challenge of the levee path each day, was an effort to reach 'instantaneity in omnipresence' before the path was ended.

Thus, from the wide scene of knowledge, and numberless experiences of remembering, there evolved a yoga of death and rebirth.

A YOGA OF DEATH AND REBIRTH

I depart from my Family, alone in freedom,
I depart from my Friend, shedding influences,
I depart from my Beloved, untouchable am I,
Into Solitude, unaccompanied, I depart:
   Bodiless now—in the Cathedral of Flesh.

I depart through its hungers, craving tastes,
I depart through the craving, wanting sustenance,
I depart through non-sustenance, utterly spent:

Bodiless I—in the Horizon of Pain.

I depart through the Pain, life draining in Sorrow,
I depart through the Sorrow into shadowy Mind,
I depart through all shadows—yet Breath remains:

Bodiless held—at the Rhythmic Gate.

I depart through non-breathing, in Fire arise,
I depart through Flamed-Being to the Radiant Whole,
I depart through that Wholeness, in Sublime Return:

Beingless now—the Power and Love in All.

From aeonian Bliss and Beingless Power,
I return through the Glory of the Radiant Whole,
I return through the Perfect, to the Limited Form:

Embodied am I—in the Self's Purest Fire.

I return from Omnipresence, to the patterned Place;
I return from the Infinite, to the sacrificial Sphere;
I return from the Many, to the Individual Man:

Embodied was I—in the Splendour of Space.

I return through the Center to the newly-born Mind,
I return through the Mind to the bondage of Desire,
I return through the Veil that obliterates the Past:

Imprisoned am I—in the Cathedral of Flesh.

I return to my own, in joyful uniting,
I return through all fears of the Chains and the Doors;
I return with fresh Vision and Courage Sublime:

Beingless Forever—the Power and the Love in All.

* * *

APPENDIX

Attempts to Prove Reincarnation

Of interest, and of great value, I feel, are the later day efforts to prove that reincarnation actually occurs. Usually these efforts are based on evidence drawn from memory of a past life that was lived recently enough that the details of memory can be substantiated by checking historical and geographical facts. Among such efforts is, notably, the work of Dr. Ian Stevenson, whose book *Twenty Cases Suggestive of Reincarnation* charts a number of careful analyses of what are apparently genuine cases of past-life memories.

Among the examples offered, is the story of Swarnlata, who was born in 1948 in Madhya Pradesh, India. At the age of 3 years she began insisting upon the truth of her vivid memories of a recent past-life. In 1961 in his investigations of relevant reports, Dr. Stevenson interviewed the child and her family, establishing a number of facts that supported her memory of a former life. This case has the added significance of Dr. Stevenson's further interviews with Swarnlata ten years later, in 1971. Meanwhile, she had obtained degrees with distinction in Botany, and now, as a mature woman, it seems that not only does she preserve the memories of her former life, but knows quite well the family of which she was a member in that life. There are visits between the two families, and Swarnlata says: "I share with them in their pleasure and pain", a remark that suggests strong feelings of a family tie. Judging from the documentation, hers is surely an authentic case of rapid rebirth.

Dr. Stevenson included the amazing case of the young Hindu girl, Shanti Devi, the press releases of which astonished the world in 1937.

Shanti Devi was born in Delhi, India. From her fourth year she began referring to incidents in her past life. She described in detail her former home, the town of Muttra in which she had lived, the names of her husband, her relatives and other friends, as well as the temple she attended, and the money she had saved and buried to donate to the temple. Shanti Devi insisted that she be taken to visit the town where she had lived before. After some years of her insistence, a letter was written to the gentleman she had named as having been her husband in her former lifetime. To everyone's surprise, this man answered the letter addressed to him, verifying as substantially true, the details in the story told by Shanti Devi. The upshot of this was that a grand uncle of Shanti Devi arranged to take her to the village. With a number of accompanying friends and relatives, she travelled to the place of her former birth. As soon as she arrived in the town, she began pointing to changes that had taken place in the past few years.

She led the way directly to her house. She had previously described correctly the house and its rooms, so upon arriving there, she indicated her own former room where she had buried the money for the temple. Upon digging in the ground, the case was located and opened, but the box was empty. The girl was very excited about this, and insisted that she had put the money there. Her former husband, who was present, admitted that he had taken the money after she had died. Shanti Devi wanted to remain with him, although she was only 11 years old; but her parents wisely insisted that she return with them to her present home and family, and her new life.

Both of these cases, and the others similar to them, raise implications that seem to diverge from the concept of reincarnation as presented in this book. Yet the cases have reasonable and intelligent explanations within the larger horizon of reincarnation, as shown in the conception of the *normal* cycle of life-after-death, which has been outlined in Chapter 4.

Numbers of such cases are turning up. It seems that in our time, which is a most unusual era of transition, innumerable children are coming back into physical incarnation without traversing the whole cycle of after-death stages. In a small pamphlet called "Reincarnation: Verified cases of Re-birth After Death"*, the compiler, Dr. Kekai Nandan Sahay, an officer of a high court, has collected a number of instances of children remembering their previous incarnations. Many detailed memories are given that have been carefully investigated, and in most cases corroborated by numbers of reputable witnesses. All these cases, however, are deviations from what is described in this book as the normal course of reincarnation. Even if thousands of such instances came to light, they would be only a tiny fraction of the thousands of millions of human beings who have lived and died on this earth, the overwhelming majority of whom must have passed through all stages of the great cycle of reincarnation. The required time for the normal rhythm, as we have seen, is much longer than the short span of years usually indicated by people who remember the details of a recent past lifetime.

Shanti Devi's reincarnation did not follow the full cycle. Moreover, as usual in these cases, no memory is brought through that sheds any light whatsoever on the known processes of reincarnation. This is a major reason why such cases must be treated cautiously as offering very limited reports concerning reincarnation. It is characteristic of them that no interest is shown in what happened after death, and during that exceedingly important period preceding rebirth. Yet, normally what happens imme-

*Mentioned in "The Rationale of Reincarnation" - A. E. Powell.

diately after death and throughout the span between life-times, is so striking, that it cannot help but be of first importance. Obviously this was not the case with Swarn-lata or Shanti Devi. Their orientation to life on earth and immediate return, was so strong that the interval experienced between death and rebirth was too inconsequential to receive conscious attention.

One of the most remarkable efforts in recent times to establish a valid case for reincarnation, was the *Bridey Murphy* inquiry. The hypnosis technique of 'age-regression' was used to evoke from the sub-conscious mind of a subject, memories in reverse order. By this technique, the subject's attention is processed backward in time to earliest childhood and infancy, then the period prior to birth. In the *Bridey Murphy* case, memory was regressed beyond birth into scenes that preceded it. The time prior to birth is of course, the same as the after-death period following one's last lifetime. Bridey Murphy's life and death took place in the not-distant past; therefore the facts elicited in the interviews could be, and were, to some extent confirmed in several important instances. Altogether, the Bridey Murphy case seemed to confirm from another line of inquiry, the reality of reincarnation.

The account of these experiments was published in the book, Morey Bernstein's *The Search for Bridey Murphy* (N.Y.: Doubleday, 1965), a businessman interested in this field of research. The procedure used, was by prompted regression of the subject in deep trance, by means of questions and answers, which were tape-recorded. It seems that in her former life, the subject was 'Bridey Murphy' who lived from 1798 - 1864 in Cork, Ireland. It was established that the Bridey Murphy of the 19th Century had reincarnated as Miss Ruth Mills in the U.S.A. in the twentieth century. During the six taped interviews, the effort was made to ascertain as many memories of objective facts as possible that were verifiable. Later, a committee in Ireland was formed for the purpose of investigating these. Although some of the incidents and descriptions were actually found to check, the complete research requirements were too formidable to undertake within the limitations that prevailed.

Characteristically, in the Bridey Murphy case, as in the others mentioned here, practically no knowledge of reincarnation was obtained. All attention was directed toward the physical facts, the least important elements concerning reincarnation. The inadequacy of the Bridey Murphy approach is shown by its revelation of the after-death state. Without deeper inquiry into the grand cycle of reincarnation, there is no explanation for the random purposelessness of the grey, mediocre situation that was reported.

When the subject was asked about Bridey Murphy's death, she remembered principally that she didn't go to purgatory "like Father John said". And when asked where did she go? she made the remarkable statement "I stayed right in that house". She said she attended her own funeral, and "watched them ditch my body". When she tried to talk to others "they wouldn't listen". She seemed greatly disturbed by this, and by her husband Brian's spiritual anxieties. When she was aked whether, in the after-death period she ever went to school, or received instructions of any kind, she said "No".

The drabness of this period is illustrated in the following excerpt, which is typical of the scenes elicited:

" . . . did you have any attachments of any kind, any family attachments, relatives?
"No".
"No marriages?"
"No".
"Do relatives stay together?"
"No, my mother never was with me, my father said he saw her, but I didn't."
"Was there any such thing as love and hate?"

"No".
"You neither loved nor hated?"
"No . . . loved those that you left".
"You said that you couldn't talk very long with anyone in that Astral world, that they would go away. Where did they go?"
"They would just . . . journey . . . you have no time . . . nothing's important."
"You said that you went from your house at Belfast in this Astral world . . . how did you get from Belfast to Cork?"
"I just willed myself there."
"Willed yourself there? How long did it take you to get from Belfast to Cork?"
"I don't know, it wasn't any time."
In other words, when you thought about being in Cork, you were there in Cork?"
"Just almost".

The Bridey Murphy experiment has special interest because it details memories of after-death existence that are apparently bona fide, yet without an application of occult knowledge about what was taking place, the descriptions alone give no sense of order and intelligent development. The experience after death becomes a depressing existence in a limbo of purposeless confusion. The aimless, random wandering is sufficiently disturbing to many people who hear of it, to turn them away from any further interest whatever in the subject of reincarnation. However, for the serious student, the Bridey Murphy case adds a wealth of incidental data of interest to all investigators of the general theory of reincarnation. By way of explanation, Bridey Murphy's situation is typical of an earthbound soul—one who remains in the earthsphere environment because of lack of interest in anything else, or because of strong cravings that hold a discarnate person there. For some karmic reason, Bridey Murphy remained attached to the physical world, and she neither continued her journey inwardly to her true astral home, nor into the heaven world beyond. In the grand cycle of reincarnation her course would have taken her out of the physical neighborhood, and would have required a much longer period of time than that mentioned in the tapes.

Another remarkable avenue of investigating reincarnation—that of clairvoyance—was opened by Edgar Cayce, who, throughout twenty years of humanitarian service, brought medical relief and healing to thousands of people through his clairvoyant-hypnosis diagnosis and advice for treatment. He had witnessed so many instances of the effects of great suffering, that he sought more deeply their causes. Thus, he began his *life-readings,* which were explorations into past lifetimes of caused relationships". *Karma* thus came into the picture, linked to series of reincarnations, and gave the *idea* of reincarnation substantial support, together with an intelligent grasp of the modus operandi of the immortal Soul in unfolding its latent spiritual powers through lifetimes spent on this earth.

In the book *Many Mansions,* by Gina Cerminara, which was inspired by what the author discovered in the files of over 2,000 life-readings by Edgar Cayce, the aspect of karma in connection with reincarnation is given special emphasis.

A great variety of individual experiences emerge from the Cayce tapes, which the author has associated in chapters under different headings, the summation being "A philosophy to live by". We agree with Dr. Cerminara that many people of the Western world who investigate these matters " . . . may find it difficult to deny that the reincarnationist view is precise, rational, and intelligible . . . "*

Another approach to this question is that of Spiritualism. It has happened occasionally that through some unusual dispensation, an arrangement between two

*Many Mansions-Gina Cerminara-p. 128.

people close to each other, one of whom has died, has made it possible to communicate in a manner such as that demonstrated in *Letters from a Living Dead Man,* by Elsa Barker. Of special interest is the account given in brief letter-form of the development of the facility used for communication. The information disclosed in *Letters from a Living Dead Man* is useful to the student who is sorting through many conflicting ideas for confirmation of his growing conception of reincarnation. Many spiritualistic sources, whilst denying the truth of reincarnation, nevertheless give valuable information about after-death situations. There are spiritualistic individuals and groups, who try to be helpful to the earth-bound persons. Some years ago a Dr. Wickland organized a "Spiritual Clinic" for this purpose. A summation of his case histories are available in the book *Thirty Years among The Dead.* I have drawn from it an excerpt illustrating the condition of a suicide: The newspapers had reported previously the suicide of a movie actress. Six days later a close friend of hers, also ended her life. These two people were brought into the spiritualistic circle in painful contortions and crying wrechedly.

> *Doctor:* "Who are you friend? . . . you have been brought here to be helped . . "
> *Spirit:* "Help me! Oh help me! . . . Give me something to drink . . . some champagne.
> *Doctor:* "You are now a spirit, and will have no further use for champagne . . . "
> *Spirit:* (writhing . . . as if in intense pain) . . . '-'Give me something to drink! . . . Take me out of this!"
> *Doctor:* "Try to be reasonable . . . Intelligent spirits can help you and bring you to a better understanding . . . "
> *Spirit:* "I want champagne, and I want it quick!"
> *Doctor:* "You won't get any more champagne; that life is past. Your earthly life is over . . . "
> *Spirit:* "Give me a cigarette!"

> *Doctor:* "Your only salvation now is to realize your condition . . . "
>
> *Spirit:* (becoming greatly excited) "Look at that man standing over there! He's horrible - horrible!" (He was the entity that caused her suicide).
>
> *Doctor:* "Listen to us; we are your friends. This is a psychic circle where we help spirits that are in darkness and ingnorance . . . Calm yourself . . . and we shall be able to help you."
>
> (Suddenly the spirit saw her friend, who also had committed suicide, and was present).
>
> *Spirit:* "Oh Anna! Anna! . . . Where did you come from? . . . She's afraid of that man too. He is going over to Anna . . . Don't let him get her!"

This was a reference to the same entity who had caused both suicides. It was only after much further calming that, with the help of servers in the Astral World, the former actress was quietened sufficiently to listen, and her fears were relieved.

> *Spirit*: " . . . I can go to sleep and rest. I am tired, and have not had any rest for years—it seems, but it is only a short time I suppose."

Two years later this same spirit returned to Dr. Wickland's circle. She was completely awakened now, and was happy in serving others. She referred to her change:

> "I was in a state of anger, and it was my death . . . I did not mean to kill myself . . . Then I woke up and saw what I had done, I was in anguish . . . if I could only tell people of the life they should live . . . it would turn many criminals, and they would become good men and women."

However, there is enough information available to clarify sensibly why it is not possible to prove the normal full cycle of reincarnation as true, with the scientific exactitude that is being sought by present methods. The theme set forth in this book suggests a rational approach in the introduction. With the firm formulation of a general theory of the rhythm of reincarnation, supported by a vast and growing collection of memories, the authenticity of which might be validated by tests such as are offered in Chapter Two, another kind of proof would appear—one that appeals to sweet reason, and heaven-born wisdom.

GLOSSARY

Absolute: The Supreme Principle and One Source of the universe. Ref. 'God'.

Akasha: The spiritual essence which pervades universal Space from densest physical matter to subtlest eternal Life.

Antahkarana: The subtle bridge of consciousness between the higher Manas and lower mental body, serving as a line of communication between the Soul and personality. It is the means (sometimes defined as an organ) by which Man transcends material mind and reaches immortal consciousness.

Archetypal (Universe): The primordial projection of the Authentic Universe that is to be evolved. It is directly created by the Third Aspect of the Logos, the potent force that drives evolution ever onward toward its goal of perfection.

Astral: The body of matter in which man experiences feeling and desire. The astral world is an invisible globe of subtle matter that surrounds and permeates the Earth.

Atma: The highest level of consciousness in man's immortal Soul. It reflects the Archetypal Lawfulness of the Universe, therefore furnishes the Soul with the quality of eternal endurance. It is the Supreme Will in Man—the Seventh Principle.

Body Elemental: The 'ethereal presence' assigned to the building and welfare of the physical body from the womb to the grave. Ref. Chapter 10,

Buddhi: The unitive principle in man's Soul that illumines the mind, transforming intellectuality into wisdom through divine love. Man uses buddhi, his Sixth Principle, to unite his consciousness with that of anything else, intuitively from within.

Causal Body: "The basis of cause"; the enduring center in which exists all causes of rebirth. It is the seat of the reincarnating Self, the true Man, the Thinker. Not an objective body, it is a center focussing the Soul, the immortal memory and the personality for any single incarnation of an individual. The Causal Body evolves through the ages.

Death: Final departure from the physical body that takes place only when the 'silver cord' is dissolved.

Devachan: Ref. 'Heaven'

Dharma: The sacred path of man's duty to the Higher Self. It is the path indicated to the Soul along which is to be achieved the next stage of unfolding. Dharma is the highest duty of an incarnation.

Divine Self, or Spirit: The original Spark that poured forth, with myriads of others, as the substance of the universe when the One became the Many. The individual Spark exists in the archetypal universe as an authentic divine Idea of you, the individual—a 'Father-in-heaven'—to which the immortal Soul aspires as it unfolds its powers through reincarnation. The divine Self is the Monad turned outward, engaged in the evolution of the universe.

Divine Trinity: Wherein the individual Self merges forever into the One. This Ultimate Trinity is composed of (a) the Archetypal Self; (b) the Monad; and (c) the Logoic Being.

Earth-bound: Those who after death try to cling to physical materiality, hence are bound to the limbo between physical and astral life.

Etheric Double: The invisible replica of the physical body, composed of the subtler physical matter beyond the gaseous stage. It is the vehicle of vitality, and the channel of communication between the physical body and the subtler astral and mental bodies.

Evil: Any form of materializing resistance or influence opposed to Life's evolution of spiritual and divine consciousness.

Evolution: The return of the Life Stream to its Source, through the unfoldment and expansion of consciousness. The evolution of bodies takes place secondarily, as the evolution of consciousness requires more efficient vehicles.

God (also *Absolute:* and *Solar Logos*): The unborn, eternal, beginningless and endless, Light-Essence, that is the Absolute Source of All, from which emanates the Universe; and with fulfillment of its purpose, returns the Perfected Creation to total Union. The Solar Logos is God the Creator of the Solar Universe. He appeared as Light in the beginning, and is a trinity of being consisting of the Light; the Substance that pervades all Space (Akasha); and the projection of the Archetypal, or Authentic Universe, from which all else proceeds. These three aspects are usually denoted as Will, Wisdom and Activity—the Triune Supreme Being.

Heaven: or Devachan, the "Shining Land". The culminating situation and period of an incarnation. Ref. Chapter 8.

Higher Self: The Higher Self is the Atma, Buddhi, Manas structure of the Soul focussed in the relationship of Manas with mortal mind. Through Manas the abstract content of the Soul can be contacted and known.

Immortal Trinity: The Manas, Buddhi, Atma levels of consciousness united as the immortal Soul.

Involution: The great cycle of Life's descent into identification with matter, the involvement of Life from the archetypal level to densest materiality. It is the reverse tide to that of evolution. Involution precedes evolution.

Karma: The universal Law of Cause and Effect. Cycles of karma are generated by every action, feeling and thought. The Law restores all energies to an equilibrium as the effect of each cause becomes fully worked out.

Manas: The immortal Mind. It operates in the three upper sub-planes of mental matter. It is the higher mental faculty which makes of man an intelligent and moral being. The pure Manas is reflective of the Divine Mind.

Mental Body: The transient vehicle for Man's mortal mind. It is composed of matter in the lower sub-planes of the mental plane, where the energies of the mind create thought-forms. It is Man's instrument for dealing with all daily activities in the material worlds.

Monad: Ref. 'Divine Self'.

Mortal Trinity: The unit of physical, astral and mental vehicles of action, feeling and thought.

Nepenthe: The veil drawn before physical birth, over all objective memory of the past.

Occult: Usually associated with the term "science", indicating the science of the hidden side of Nature. In its broadest sense the occult includes not only invisible Nature, but all the psychic as well as subtlest spiritual levels of Life and consciousness.

Psychometry: Reading or seeing with the *inner sight*. The word literally means "Soul-measuring", the science of psychometry is far more subtle than the technical definition that describes what clairvoyants or sensitives and parapsychologists usually ascribe to it. Psychometry also includes, for example, 'touch' at the Egoic level, with whatever is examined. Ordinarily, in the popular usage, it means to perceive information through the means of touching some object.

Physical Body: The transient vehicle of man's seven principles which are: Physical body, Etheric double, Astral body, Mental body(mortal), Manas (higher mind), Buddhi, Atma.

Seven Planes of the Universe: Beginning with the highest Spiritual first plane, they are: Adi, Anupadaka, Atmic, Buddhic, Mental, Astral, Physical. Each is said to consist of seven sub-planes. In the densest physical plane, the sub-divisions are recognizable as solid matter, liquid, gaseous and other four invisible etheric levels that transmit sound, light and electrical impulses.

Sex: Ref. Chapter 11.

Silver Cord: Between the physical body and the etheric double there is a glistening, delicate cord referred to by occultists as the "silver cord". The actual moment of death occurs when this delicate cord snaps, because the withdrawal of the etheric double has broken the last link that Man's higher consciousness has with the physical body.

Solar Logos: Ref. 'God'.

Soul: The immortal Being that unites the Atma, Buddhi, Manas levels of consciousness in a single all-surveying intelligence. The Soul at the Manas level is the reincarnating Self; at the Buddhic level it is the Space vehicle of Atma; at the Atmic level it is the power that reflects and channels Lawfulness, and other aspects of the Will that created the universe.

Tanha: Thirst for life renewed in physical form.

CLARIFICATION OF TERMS USED TO DESIGNATE SUCCESSIVE LIFETIMES

Several terms are used synonymously to designate the general idea of reincarnation. But they do not have the same precise meaning. The terms are as follows:

Reincarnation: Re-enfleshment, or rebirth into the physical world in a new human body, after a period of existence in the immaterial or spiritual condition between incarnations. The idea implies that there is an immortal element of self-consciousness in the nature of Man, that survives the death of the physical body. Reincarnation suggests larger purpose—that the growth of the immortal Self takes place through stages of incarnations in human bodies. Reincarnation can be viewed as a law in Nature, that provides man with a physical body appropriate to his stage of growth. The non-dying elements and the transient physical body are brought together in a tandem convenience for the purpose of spiritual growth toward a far-off divine end.

Transmigration: A term often used in place of reincarnation but it does not have the same meaning. 'Trans' means to pass over, beyond, through; 'migration' means to move from one place to another. Together, they signify 'to pass from one body to another body at death'. This has an implication of immediacy—an immediate transference from one body to another. This word is employed also to convey the idea of passage into bodies that are not necessarily human. There are many adherents to the general idea of reincarnation, who hold the belief that human beings sometimes transmigrate into animal bodies. But such random descent into lower kingdoms of nature is held to be impossible in the terms of evolution designated by the grand cycle of reincarnation.

Metempsychosis: Derives from the Greek idea of the passing of the psyche, or soul, at death, into another body. Here again, we have a term that expresses randomness of purpose. It is certainly not synonymous with the rhythmic cycle implied by the word reincarnation.

Paligenesis: Sometimes used to indicate the doctrine of successive births, but it more accurately conveys the meaning of resurrection, or regeneration of a form in order to re-embody it. It's synonyms are 'revivification' and 'resurrection'.

Pre-Existence: Does not necessarily mean reincarnation. Existence 'before' can be before anytime prior to the present time, and anywhere, whether in spiritual or physical realms.

Recurring Earth Lives: This expression is more nearly synonymous with reincarnation.

Rebirth: The word does not indicate precisely birth in a new physical body. Rebirth can occur mentally or emotionally as well. Whenever an individual opens a new range of experience, or attains an expansion of consciousness, he is 'reborn'.

The word **Immortal** is often associated with the idea of reincarnation. An awareness of immortality is the natural concomitant of recollecting the permanency of one's Self throughout the cycles of death and rebirth. The individual Self in man actually experiences immortality, even though some part of his familiar being is lost in the processes that follow death of the physical body.

REINCARNALIA

The first step toward obtaining a general background knowledge of views and comments on the subject of reincarnation, is to secure, if possible, an anthology of statements that have been made by recognized authorities and notable people, whose views have value. Such a compilation has been assembled by Joseph Head and S. L. Cranston, in their useful volume *Reincarnation–an East-West Anthology*. In addition to the selection of pertinent material, the wide references to sources and authors are themselves suggestive of where one might pursue further investigation into what is known and thought about reincarnation.

The following list of books contain useful information on reincarnation:

Arundale, Francesca. *The Idea of Rebirth.*

Bendit, Laurence J. *The Mirror of Life and Death.* Wheaton: Theosophical Publishing House, 1967.

Bernstein, Morey. *The Search for Bridey Murphy.* New York: Doubleday, 1965.

Besant, Annie. *Man and His Bodies.* Chicago: Theosophical Press, 1923.

―――. *Reincarnation.* Adyar, India: Theosophical Publishing House, 1970.

―――. *The Seven Principles of Man.* London: Theosophical Publishing House, 1918.

―――. *Karma.* Krotona: Theosophical Publishing House, 1918.

―――. *The Ancient Wisdom.* Adyar, India: Theosophical Publishing House, 1966.

―――. *Death and After.* Adyar, India: Theosophical Publishing House, 1952.

―――. *Popular Lectures on Theosophy.*

Blavatsky, H. P. *The Key to Theosophy.* Pasadena: Theosophical University Press, 1946.

Cerminara, Gina. *Many Mansions*. New York: William Sloan Associates, 1950.

Challoner, H. K. *The Wheel of Rebirth*. London: Theosophical Publishing House, 1969.

Ebon, Martin, ed. *Reincarnation in the Twentieth Century*. New York: National American Library, 1970.

Hall, Manly P. *Reincarnation: The Cycle of Necessity*. Los Angeles: Philosophical Research Society, 1946.

Hanson, Virginia, ed. *Karma: The Universal Law of Harmony*. Wheaton: Theosophical Publishing House, 1975.

Head, J., and Cranston, S. L., comps. *Reincarnation: An East-West Anthology*. Wheaton: Theosophical Publishing House, 1975.

Hodson, Geoffrey. *Reincarnation: Fact or Fallacy?* Wheaton: Theosophical Publishing House, 1967.

Jinarajadasa, C. *How We Remember Our Past Lives*. Adyar, India: Theosophical Publishing House, 1915.

Judge, W. Q. *The Ocean of Theosophy*. Los Angeles: United Lodge of Theosophists, 1928.

Kubler-Ross, Elizabeth. *Questions and Answers on Death and Dying*. New York: Macmillan, 1974.

_____. *On Death and Dying*. New York: Macmillan Publishing Company, 1969.

Langley, Noel. *Edgar Cayce on Reincarnation*. New York: Castle Books, 1967.

Leadbeater, C. W. *The Other Side of Death*. Adyar, India: Theosophical Publishing House, 1961.

_____. *The Astral Plane*. Adyar, India: Theosophical Publishing House, 1970.

_____. *The Devachanic Plane*. London: Theosophical Publishing House, 1909.

Leek, Sybil. *Reincarnation: The Second Chance*. New York: Stein & Day, 1974.

Pearson, E. Norman. *Space, Time and Self*. Adyar, India: Theosophical Publishing House, 1957.

Perkins, James S. *Through Death to Rebirth*. Wheaton: Theosophical Publishing House, 1961.

Powell, A. E. *The Rationale of Reincarnation*.

————. *The Etheric Double.* Wheaton: Theosophical Publishing House, 1975.

————. *The Astral Body.* London: Theosophical Publishing House, 1972.

————. *The Mental Body.* London: Theosophical Publishing House, 1975.

————. *The Causal Body.* London: Theosophical Publishing House, 1928.

Reyes, Benito F. *Scientific Evidence of the Existence of the Soul.* Wheaton: Theosophical Publishing House, 1970.

Ryall, E. W. *Second Time Round.*

Santesson, Hans Stefan. *Reincarnation.*

Sinnett, A. P. *The Growth of the Soul.* New York: Theosophical Publishing House, 1905.

————. *Occult Essays.* London: Theosophical Publishing Society, 1905.

————. *Mahatma Letters,* 3rd. and revised ed. Adyar, India: Theosophical Publishing House, 1962.

Stevenson, Dr. Ian. *Twenty Cases Suggestive of Reincarnation.* New York: American Society for Psychical Research, 1966.

Walker, E. D. *Reincarnation: A Study of Forgotten Truth.*

Wickland, Carl. *Thirty Years Among The Dead.* California: Newcastle Publishing, 1974.

Wright, Leoline L. *Reincarnation: A Lost Chord in Modern Thought.* Wheaton: Theosophical Publishing House, 1975.

INDEX

Other Quest books about reincarnation

CATHARS AND REINCARNATION
By Arthur Guirdham
An English girl remembers her 13th century life as a heretic.

REINCARNATION
By Leoline L. Wright
What reincarnates and why don't we remember?

REINCARNATION: EAST WEST ANTHOLOGY
Comp. by Joseph Head and S.L. Cranston
Comments from over 400 world famous people on this concept

REINCARNATION: FACT OR FALLACY?
By Geoffrey Hodson
An inquiry into the evidence for the rebirth theory.

REINCARNATION IN CHRISTIANITY
By Geddes MacGregor
Is the rebirth concept compatible with Christian dogma?

THROUGH DEATH TO REBIRTH
By James S. Perkins
A study of the nature and method of reincarnation.

WHEEL OF REBIRTH
By H.K. Challoner
An autobiographical account of the author's past lives.

These titles are available from:
QUEST BOOKS
306 West Geneva Road
Wheaton, Illinois 60187